THE OBSERVER'S
POCKET SERIES
. . .

THE OBSERVER'S BOOK
OF AIRCRAFT ↶ ↶

The Observer's Books

THE OBSERVER'S BOOK OF

AIRCRAFT

Compiled by
WILLIAM GREEN

With silhouettes by
DENNIS PUNNETT

Describing
153   AIRCRAFT
with 279 illustrations

1969 Edition

FREDERICK WARNE & CO. LTD.
FREDERICK WARNE & CO. INC.

LONDON · NEW YORK

© FREDERICK WARNE & CO. LTD.
LONDON, ENGLAND
1969

Eighteenth Edition 1969

LIBRARY OF CONGRESS CATALOG CARD NO. 57-4425

Recommended by
THE AIR SCOUTS' DEPARTMENT
of
THE BOY SCOUTS' ASSOCIATION

7232 1032 2
Printed in Great Britain

INTRODUCTION TO THE 1969 EDITION

As this volume of *The Observer's Book of Aircraft*—the 18th annual edition—is passed for press, the Anglo-French Concorde was performing final taxying trials and had just been beaten by the Soviet Tu-144 by a short head in the race to gain the prestige of being the first supersonic transport to take to the air; the world's largest airliner, the mighty Boeing 747, was poised for flight, with commercial service scheduled for the end of 1969, while, representative of a new generation of Soviet airliners, the Tu-154 had attained its early flight test phase. Further down the commercial size scale, the little Beriev Be-30 feederliner had flown with its definitive engines, and was expected to enter Aeroflot service during the course of the year; the competitive Czechoslovak L 410 Turbolet had attained an advanced stage of construction, and, on the other side of the Atlantic, the Metro commuterliner was scheduled to commence testing shortly after the appearance of this volume.

On the military side, the largest military transport, the C-5A Galaxy, was well advanced in its flight trials with first deliveries scheduled for mid-1969; prototypes of the Anglo-French Jaguar tactical support aircraft were under test in France; the production life of the Atlantic maritime patrol aircraft had been extended by orders from the Netherlands and Italy; and the Harrier, the world's first production V/STOL fighter, was being readied for its 1969 début in R.A.F. service, as was also the Nimrod patrol aircraft, and the Phantom F.G.R. Mk. 2, the British services' version of the versatile McDonnell F-4, which, by the beginning of 1969, was entering Iranian service in its F-4D form, had found customers in Federal Germany and Israel, and had been selected for licence manufacture in Japan.

These and many other new aircraft of 18 countries are described in this edition of *The Observer's Book of Aircraft*. Seventy per cent of the 126 detailed three-view general-arrangement silhouettes are either updated or entirely new to this edition, and I should like to record my thanks to John W. R. Taylor, editor of *Jane's All the World's Aircraft*, and Gordon Swanborough, editor of *Flying Review International*, for assistance in obtaining some of the 153 photographs appearing on the following pages. I should also like to acknowledge the following sources of photographs: AiReview of Japan (pages 30, 148, 170, 204, 262); Howard Levy (pages 10 and 260); Ronaldo S. Olive (page 8), and Stephen P. Peltz (pages 44, 112, 146, 208, 240, 278 and 283).

WILLIAM GREEN

AERMACCHI M.B.326G

Country of Origin: Italy.

Type: Tandem Two-seat Basic Trainer and Single- or Two-seat Light Counter-Insurgency Aircraft.

Power Plant: One Rolls-Royce Bristol Viper 20 Mk. 540 turbojet rated at 3,410 lb.s.t.

Performance: (Trainer at 8,455 lb.) Maximum speed, 524 m.p.h. at 20,000 ft.; maximum cruising speed, 495 m.p.h.; initial climb rate 6,050 ft./min.; service ceiling, 47,000 ft.; range (8% reserves), 1,278 mls., (with two 52·5 Imp. gal. auxiliary tanks), 1,544 mls.

Weights: (Trainer) Normal loaded, 8,455 lb.; ferry, 9,555 lb.; (armed—one pilot), max. 10,500 lb.

Armament: Four hardpoints each stressed to carry 1,000 lb. and two hardpoints stressed for 750 lb. Six 100-, 250-, or 500-lb. bombs, four 750-lb. M-117 bombs, four 500- or 750-lb. napalm tanks, two Sidewinder AAMs, two Nord AS.11 or AS.12 ASMs, two M-3 0·5-in., or six SUU 11/A 7·62 mm. gun pods.

Status: (M.B.326G) First of two prototypes flown May 9, 1967. In production with initial batch of six ordered 1968 (as M.B.326K) for Argentine Navy.

Notes: Prototype M.B. 326 flown December 10, 1957. All earlier production models have 2,500 lb.s.t. Viper 22-1 (see 1966 edition). One hundred delivered to Italian Air Force, eight to Tunisia (M.B.326B), four to Alitalia (M.B.326D), and seven to Ghana (M.B.326F). Initial order for 75 placed by R.A.A.F. for M.B.326H version of which 30th and subsequent of entirely indigenous manufacture. S.A.A.F. acquiring 234 licence-built M.B.326M as Atlas Impala II.

6

AERMACCHI M.B.326G

Dimensions: Span, 35 ft. 7¼ in.; length, 34 ft. 11¼ in.; height, 12 ft. 2½ in.; wing area, 208·3 sq. ft.

AEROTEC 122 UIRAPURU

Country of Origin: Brazil.

Type: Two-seat Light Basic Trainer.

Power Plant: One Lycoming O-320-A (pre-production) or O-320-B2B (production) four-cylinder horizontally-opposed engine rated at 150 h.p. (A) or 160 h.p. (B2B).

Performance: (Pre-production) Maximum speed, 149 m.p.h. at sea level; maximum cruising speed (75% power), 130 m.p.h. at 5,000 ft.; economical cruising speed (65% power), 124 m.p.h.

Weights: (Pre-production) Empty, 1,135 lb.; maximum loaded, 1,852 lb.

Accommodation: Individual side-by-side seats with full dual controls. A 220-lb. capacity baggage compartment aft of seats.

Status: First of two prototypes flown June 2, 1965, first of two pre-production aircraft flown January 23, 1968, and initial deliveries against production contract for 30 aircraft begun late 1968.

Notes: The Uirapuru has been developed by the Sociedade Aerotec to meet a Brazilian Air Force requirement for a successor to the Brazilian-built Fokker S.11 and S.12 trainers currently serving at the *Escola de Aeronáutica* at Pirassununga, and has been adopted under the designation T-23. The Uirapuru is of all-metal construction, and the pre-production (illustrated above) and production models differ from the prototypes in having a redesigned cockpit canopy, adjustable seats and stick-type control columns.

8

AEROTEC 122 UIRAPURU

Dimensions: Span, 28 ft. 6½ in.; length, 21 ft. 5 in.; height, 8 ft. 1 in.; wing area, 144·6 sq. ft.

AMERICAN AVIATION AA-1 YANKEE

Country of Origin: U.S.A.

Type: Two-seat Light Cabin Monoplane.

Power Plant: One Lycoming O-235-C2C four-cylinder horizontally-opposed engine rated at 108 h.p.

Performance: Maximum speed, 144 m.p.h. at sea level; cruising speed (75% power), 135 m.p.h. at 8,000 ft.; range at economical cruise, 512 mls.; initial climb rate, 830 ft./min.; service ceiling, 11,200 ft.

Weights: Empty, 940 lb.; loaded, 1,500 lb.

Accommodation: Two seats side by side beneath aft-sliding transparent canopy.

Status: First prototype flown July 11, 1963 (as Bede BD-1), flying in redesigned form on March 2, 1967. Production initiated by American Aviation with 50 delivered by beginning of 1969 when production was six per week.

Notes: The AA-1 Yankee has been developed from the BD-1 by the American Aviation Corporation (formerly Bede Aviation Corporation), the production model retaining the bonded metal honeycomb panel fuselage construction but differing from the definitive BD-1 prototype in having a wider-track undercarriage, the original sprung-steel legs being supplanted by shorter legs of laminated fibreglass; redesigned vertical tail surfaces, and a modified wing with Hoerner tips and equal-span flaps and ailerons. The Yankee is offered in three versions: the Yankee Standard with basic instrumentation, the Yankee Trader with limited radio, and the Yankee Clipper with complete IFR equipment.

AMERICAN AVIATION AA-1 YANKEE

Dimensions: Span, 24 ft. 5½ in.; length, 19 ft. 2¾ in.; height, 6 ft. 5¾ in.; wing area, 98·11 sq. ft.

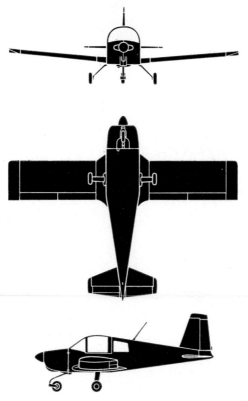

ANTONOV AN-22 ANTEI (COCK)

Country of Origin: U.S.S.R.

Type: Long-range Military and Commercial Freighter.

Power Plants: Four Kuznetsov NK-12MA turboprops each rated at 15,000 e.h.p.

Performance: Maximum speed, 460 m.p.h.; maximum cruising speed, 422 m.p.h.; cruising altitude, 26,250–32,800 ft.; range (with 99,208-lb. payload), 6,835 mls. at 373 m.p.h., (with 176,370-lb. payload), 3,107 mls. at 404 m.p.h.

Weights: Empty equipped, 251,327 lb.; maximum loaded, 551,156 lb.

Accommodation: Crew of 5–6 and cabin for 28–29 passengers between freight hold and flight deck. Freight hold can accommodate three tracked carriers for single Frog or twin Ganef surface-to-surface missiles, self-propelled guns, etc.

Status: First of five prototypes flown February 27, 1965. Two prototypes delivered to Soviet Air Force and three to Aeroflot. First production aircraft (for Soviet Air Force) flown spring 1967. Production for commercial operation envisaged as 30 per year from 1968.

Notes: The An-22 was designed primarily to meet a Soviet Air Force requirement for a heavy strategic transport, and possessed the distinction of being the world's largest aircraft until the appearance of the C-5A Galaxy. By late 1968 it was known to be in service with several Sov. A.F. units. A modified version for Aeroflot actively under development late 1968 will provide accommodation for 300–350 passengers and 66,140 lb. freight, this load being carried over 1,865 miles.

ANTONOV AN-22 ANTEI (COCK)

Dimensions: Span, 211 ft. 3½ in.; length 189 ft. 8 in.;
height, 41 ft. 0 in.; wing area, 5,166·68 sq. ft.

ANTONOV AN-24 SRS. 2 (COKE)

Country of Origin: U.S.S.R.

Type: Short- to Medium-range Commercial Transport.

Power Plants: Two Ivchenko Al-24T turboprops each rated at 2,820 e.s.h.p. and (An-24RV) one Tumanskii RU-19-300 turbojet rated at 1,980 lb.s.t.

Performance: Maximum speed, 335 m.p.h. at 19,685 ft.; maximum cruising speed, 311 m.p.h.; economical cruising speed, 280 m.p.h. at 19,680 ft.; range (with maximum payload—12,125 lb.), 400 mls., (with maximum fuel and 5,372-lb. payload), 1,550 mls.; initial climb rate, 1,480 ft./min.

Weights: Maximum loaded (An-24V Srs. 2) 45,540 lb., (An-24RV), 48,000 lb.

Accommodation: (An-24V Srs. 2) Various arrangements possible for maximum of 50 passengers in high-density layout. (An-24TV) Quick-change version with convertible freight hold with rear-loading facilities, freight conveyor rails, electric hoist, and maximum freight capacity of 12,125 lb.

Status: An-24 Series 2 in production from January 1968. First prototype An-24 flown April 1960, and second prototype plus five pre-production An-24s completed 1961. First production deliveries 1962.

Notes: An-24V Srs. 2 supplants Srs. 1 which has 2,550 e.s.h.p. Al-24 turboprops. An-24RV has auxiliary turbojet in starboard engine nacelle, and An-24TV (illustrated opposite) has air-openable rear freight hatch and twin ventral strakes.

14

ANTONOV AN-24 SRS. 2 (COKE)

Dimensions: Span, 95 ft. 10 in.; length, 77 ft. 2½ in.; height, 27 ft. 4 in.; wing area, 779·845 sq. ft.

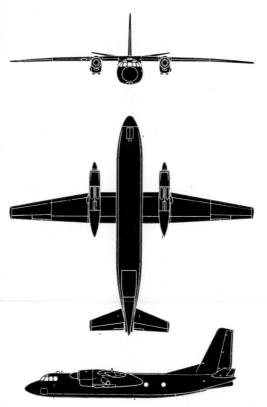

BAC ONE-ELEVEN SERIES 500

Country of Origin: United Kingdom.

Type: Short- to Medium-range Commercial Transport.

Power Plants: Two Rolls-Royce Spey 25 Mk. 512–14DW turbofans each rated at 12,460 lb.s.t.

Performance: Maximum cruising speed, 541 m.p.h. at 25,000 ft.; long-range cruising speed, 472 m.p.h. at 35,000 ft.; range with maximum payload (23,405 lb.) and nil reserves, 1,850 mls. at 35,000 ft.; range with maximum fuel, nil reserves and zero payload, 2,885 mls.

Weights: Basic operational, 54,595 lb.; maximum take-off, 98,000 lb.

Accommodation: Basic flight crew of two and high-density seating for 109 passengers. Typical mixed-class seating for 12 first-class and 79 coach-class passengers.

Status: In production with first delivery (to BEA) on August 29, 1968. Aerodynamic prototype flown on June 30, 1967.

Notes: By comparison with predecessors (see 1967 edition), the Series 500 features uprated engines, a 13 ft. 6 in. increase in overall length, and a redesigned wing with re-profiled leading edge, bigger tips increasing span and area by 5 ft. and 51 sq. ft. respectively, and modified flap-track fairings. With the Series 500 wing and similar uprated engines, the shorter-fuselage Series 400 becomes the Series 475 for hot and high environments, and a proposed development is the 130-passenger Series 600 with aft-fan derivatives of the Spey. The Series 500 serves with BEA as the Super One-Eleven.

16

BAC ONE-ELEVEN SERIES 500

Dimensions: Span, 93 ft. 6 in.; length, 107 ft. 0 in.; height, 24 ft. 6 in.; wing area, 1,031 sq. ft.

BAC LIGHTNING F. MK. 53

Country of Origin: United Kingdom.

Type: Single-seat Interceptor, Strike and Reconnaissance Fighter.

Power Plants: Two Rolls-Royce RB.146 Avon 302-C turbojets each rated at 11,100 lb.s.t. and 16,300 lb.s.t. with afterburning.

Performance: (Estimated) Maximum speed, 1,500 m.p.h. at 40,000 ft. (Mach 2·27); long-range cruising speed, 595 m.p.h. at 36,000–40,000 ft.; initial climb rate, 50,000 ft./min.; time to 40,000 ft. 2·5 min.

Weights: Estimated maximum loaded, 50,000 lb.

Armament: Interchangeable packs containing the equipment for two Red Top or Firestreak AAMs, or 44 2-in. rockets, plus two 30-mm. Aden cannon with 120 r.p.g. in ventral pack, plus two 1,000-lb. bombs or two MATRA 155 launchers for 18 SNEB 68-mm. rockets.

Status: First F. Mk. 53 flown November 1, 1966, and first delivery (Royal Saudi A.F.) on December 4, 1967. In production for Saudi Arabia and Kuwait.

Notes: Multi-mission export version of F. Mk. 6 interceptor for R.A.F. (see 1968 edition). Provision for two 260 Imp. gal. overwing ferry tanks. Developed version (illustrated opposite) can carry twin MATRA 155 launchers on each underwing pylon, plus twin MATRA launchers (each with 18 SNEB rockets and 50 Imp. gal. fuel) on overwing pylons, giving total of 144 68-mm. rockets. Alternatively two 1,000-lb. bombs may be carried on each underwing pylon plus one on each overwing pylon. Reconnaissance packs may be fitted.

BAC LIGHTNING F. MK. 53

Dimensions: Span, 34 ft. 10 in.; length (including probe), 55 ft. 3 in.; height, 19 ft. 7 in.; approximate wing area, 460 sq. ft.

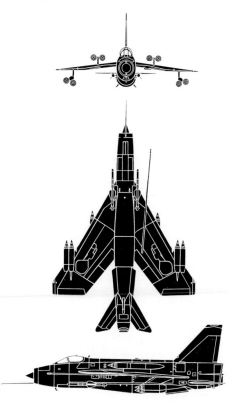

BAC 167 STRIKEMASTER

Country of Origin: United Kingdom.

Type: Side-by-side Two-seat Basic Trainer and Light Attack and Counter-insurgency Aircraft.

Power Plant: One Rolls-Royce Bristol Viper 535 (20-F.20) turbojet rated at 3,410 lb.s.t.

Performance: Maximum speed, 481 m.p.h. at 20,000 ft.; initial climb rate (at 10,823 lb.), 3,200 ft./min.; time to 20,000 ft. (at 10,823 lb.), 9 min.; range (for navigational training at 8,940 lb. with 10% reserves), 985 mls.; tactical radius (with four MATRA rocket pods, 48 Imp. gal. wingtip tank and 7 min. over target), 253 mls., (with two MATRA pods, wingtip tanks, two 75 Imp. gal. underwing tanks), 449 mls. (with wingtip and four 75 Imp. gal. tanks), 628 mls.

Weights: Empty, 5,850 lb.; loaded (pilot training), 8,050 lb., (navigational training with wingtip tanks), 8,940 lb., (two guns, four MATRA pods and tip tanks), 10,823 lb.; maximum loaded, 11,500 lb.

Armament: Two 7·62-mm. F.N. machine guns with 590 r.p.g., plus four MATRA 155 pods each with 18 SNEB 68-mm. rockets, four pods each with 36 2-in. rockets, 32 80-mm. rockets, or four 500-lb. bombs.

Status: First flown October 26, 1967. In production. First deliveries late 1968.

Notes: The Strikemaster is essentially similar to the BAC 145 Jet Provost T.5 (see 1966 edition) but employs a more powerful engine. Strikemasters are being delivered to the Saudi, Sudanese, Muscat and Oman, Kuwaiti and Singapore air arms.

BAC 167 STRIKEMASTER

Dimensions: Span, 35 ft. 4 in., (over tip tanks), 36 ft. 11 in.; length, 33 ft. 7½ in.; height, 10 ft. 2 in.; wing area, 213·7 sq. ft.

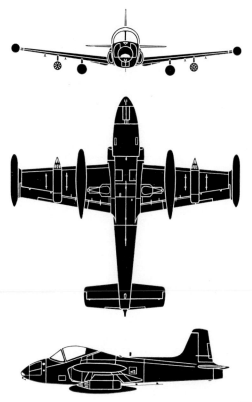

BAC VC10 C. MK. 1

Country of Origin: United Kingdom.

Type: Military Strategic Transport.

Power Plants: Four Rolls-Royce Conway R.Co.43 Conway Mk. 301 turbofans each rated at 22,500 lb.s.t.

Performance: Maximum speed, 580 m.p.h. at 30,000 ft. (Mach 0·86); normal cruising speed, 518 m.p.h. at 38,000 ft.; range (with max. payload—57,400 lb.), 3,900 mls. at 425 m.p.h. at 30,000 ft.; (with max. fuel and 24,000-lb. payload), 5,370 mls.

Weights: Operational empty, 146,000 lb.; maximum loaded, 322,000 lb.

Accommodation: A maximum of 150 troops in rear-ward-facing triple-trooping seats plus up to 19,040 lb. equipment. For the aero-medical evacuation role up to 78 casualty stretchers plus six medical and two cabin attendants may be accommodated.

Status: First VC10 C. Mk. 1 flown November 26, 1965. Total of 14 ordered (R.A.F. Air Support Command) and first delivery July 7, 1966. Production completed late 1968.

Notes: A hybrid of the Standard and Super VC10s, dimensionally similar to the former but possessing the uprated engines and fuel-carrying fin of the latter, the VC10 C. Mk. 1 is equipped with a roller freight-handling system and a new integrally machined freight floor which can take up to eight pre-loaded pallets. The VC10 currently serves with No. 10 Squadron of R.A.F. Air Support Command.

BAC VC10 C. Mk. 1

Dimensions: Span, 146 ft. 2 in.; length (including flight refuelling probe), 166 ft. 1 in.; height, 40 ft. 0 in.; wing area, 2,932 sq. ft.

BAC/SUD-AVIATION CONCORDE

Countries of Origin: United Kingdom and France.

Type: Long-haul Supersonic Commercial Transport.

Power Plants: Four Rolls-Royce Bristol/SNECMA Olympus 593 Stage O turbojets each rated at 32,825 lb.s.t. and 37,420 lb.s.t. with afterburning.

Performance: (Estimated) Maximum cruising speed, 1,350–1,385 m.p.h. (Mach 2·05–2·1) at 55,000–62,000 ft.; range with maximum fuel, nil reserves and 19,800-lb. payload, 5,595 mls.; range with maximum payload (nominal 28,000 lb.) and nil reserves, 5,215 mls. at 58,000 ft. (Mach 2·1); range with maximum payload and FAA reserves, 4,155 mls.

Weights: Basic operational, 166,200 lb.; maximum take-off, 376,000 lb.

Accommodation: Maximum high-density seating for 144 passengers, and typical mixed-class arrangement for 12 first-class and 102 coach-class passengers.

Status: First and second prototypes rolled out on December 11, 1967 (at Toulouse) and September 12, 1968 (at Filton) and, at the time of closing for press, expected to fly in January and February 1969 respectively. First (at Filton) and second (at Toulouse) pre-production aircraft scheduled to fly summer 1970.

Notes: Changes to be introduced by pre-production aircraft (described above) will include increase in overall length to 193 ft., a stepped fuselage nose and redesigned visor, and wider-chord wingtips. Airworthiness certification is scheduled for 1971, and Stage 1 engines with non-augmented rating of 35,080 lb.s.t. will be introduced after two years of operation.

24

BAC/SUD-AVIATION CONCORDE

Dimensions: (Prototypes) Span, 83 ft. 10 in.; length, 184 ft. 2 in.; height, 38 ft. 0 in.; wing area, 3,856 sq. ft.

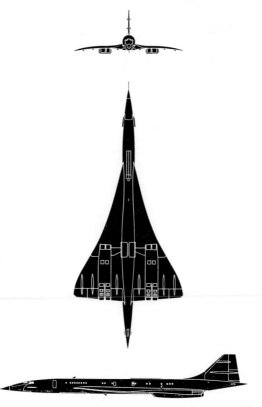

BEAGLE B.121 PUP

Country of Origin: United Kingdom.
Type: (Pup-100) Two- or (Pup-150) Two/three-seat
Light Cabin Monoplane.
Power Plant: One (Pup-100) Rolls-Royce Continental
O-200A or (Pup-150) Lycoming O-320-A2B four-
cylinder horizontally-opposed engine rated at 100 h.p.
and 150 h.p. respectively.
Performance: (Specification relates to Pup-100 with
figures in parentheses applying to the Pup-150) Maximum speed, 124 (138) m.p.h. at sea level; cruising
speed at 65% power, 108 (126) m.p.h. at 8,000 (10,000)
ft.; range with 24 Imp. gal., 502 (397) mls. at 8,000
(10,000) ft., with 34 Imp. gal., (690) mls.; initial
climb rate, 570 (840) ft./min.; service ceiling, 11,200
(14,000) ft.
Weights: Empty, 980 (1,100) lb.; maximum loaded,
1,600 (1,900) lb.
Accommodation: Side-by-side seats for two persons
with baggage space aft for 85 (120) lb. An optional
third seat is available for the Pup-150.
Status: In production, with 100 scheduled for completion by March 1969 and a further 200 by the end of
the year when output is expected to attain one per day.
Prototype Pup-100 flown April 8, 1967 and prototype
Pup-150 on October 4, 1967.
Notes: The Pup-160 is a proposed military version with
a 160 h.p. engine, a 6g structure, and sliding clear-
vision canopy.

26

BEAGLE B.121 PUP

Dimensions: Span, 31 ft. 0 in.; length, 22 ft. 11 in. (23 ft. 2 in.); height, 7 ft. 6¼ in.; wing area, 119·5 sq. ft.

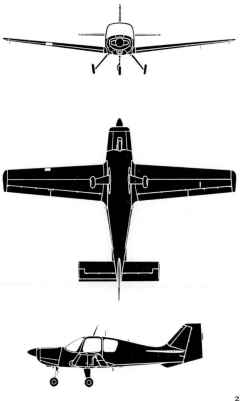

BEECHCRAFT BONANZA MODEL 36

Country of Origin: U.S.A.

Type: Six-seat Light Utility Cabin Monoplane.

Power Plant: One Continental IO-520-B six-cylinder horizontally-opposed engine rated at 285 h.p.

Performance: Maximum speed, 204 m.p.h. at sea level; cruising speed (75% power), 195 m.p.h. at 6,500 ft., (65% power), 187 m.p.h. at 10,000 ft., (55% power), 167 m.p.h. at 10,000 ft.; range (41 Imp. gal.), 530 mls. at 55% power, 485 mls. at 75% power, (66·6 Imp. gal.), 980 mls. at 55% power, 875 mls. at 75% power; initial climb rate, 1,015 ft./min.; service ceiling, 16,000 ft.

Weights: Empty equipped, 1,980 lb.; maximum loaded, 3,600 lb.

Accommodation: Six persons in pairs of individual seats plus stowage for 400 lb. baggage. Rapid conversion to utility configuration provided by two removable seats and two folding seats.

Status: In production. Introduced June 1968.

Notes: Distinguished from previous Bonanzas by conventional tail assembly in place of earlier Vee-type tail retained by current Turbo Bonanza and V35A Bonanza. Simultaneously with the appearance of the Model 36, the E33 and E33A Debonair (with similar tail assembly to Model 36) were renamed E33 and E33A Bonanzas, these being joined by the aerobatic E33B and E33C in August 1968.

BEECHCRAFT BONANZA MODEL 36

Dimensions: Span, 32 ft. 10 in.; length, 26 ft. 4 in.;
height, 9 ft. 4 in.; wing area, 177·6 sq. ft.

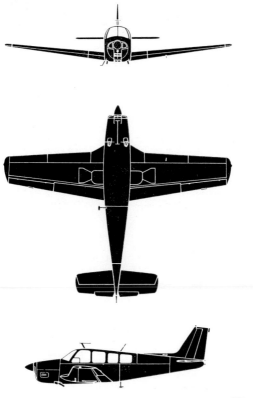

BEECHCRAFT MODEL 99

Country of Origin: U.S.A.

Type: Light Commercial Feederliner.

Power Plant: Two Pratt & Whitney PT6A-20 turbo-props each rated at 550 s.h.p.

Performance: Maximum cruising speed, 254 m.p.h. at 8,000 ft., 252 m.p.h. at 12,000 ft.; long-range cruising speed, 234 m.p.h. at 10,000 ft.; range with maximum fuel (and 1,850-lb. payload), 956 mls. at 256 m.p.h. at 12,000 ft.; range with maximum payload (3,000 lb.), 450 mls. at 256 m.p.h. at 12,000 ft.; initial climb rate (at 10,400 lb.), 1,700 ft./min.; service ceiling, 23,650 ft.

Weights: Empty equipped, 5,675 lb.; maximum loaded, 10,400 lb.

Accommodation: Flight crew of two with maximum of 15 passengers. Seats may be removed to provide cargo space, and movable bulkhead may be installed to provide separate passenger and freight compartments. A 10-seat executive version is available.

Status: In production. Prototype flown July 1966, and first production delivery effected on May 2, 1968, with more than 25 scheduled for delivery by the beginning of 1969.

Notes: A hybrid employing the wings of the Queen Air, the engines and nacelles of the King Air, sub-systems from both types, and a number of original features, the Model 99 is unpressurised, and is intended for the third-level scheduled-service market. During the course of 1969, the Model 99 will be offered with the 652 s.h.p. PT6A-27 turboprop.

30

BEECHCRAFT MODEL 99

Dimensions: Span, 45 ft. 10½ in.; length, 44 ft. 6¾ in.;
height, 14 ft. 4⅛ in.; wing area, 279·7 sq. ft.

BERIEV BE-12 (MAIL)

Country of Origin: U.S.S.R.

Type: Maritime Patrol and Reconnaissance Amphibian.

Power Plants: Two Ivchenko AI-20M turboprops each rated at 4,190 s.h.p.

Performance: (Estimated) Maximum speed, 380 m.p.h.; normal patrol speed, 200–250 m.p.h. at 5,000 ft.; initial climb rate, 3,000 ft./min.; service ceiling, 37,000 ft.; maximum range, 2,500 mls.

Weights: Approximate loaded, 60,000–65,000 lb.

Status: In production and in service.

Notes: Reportedly flown in prototype form in 1960, the Be-12 is the successor to the piston-engined Be-6 with Soviet maritime patrol units, and follows closely the basic configuration of its predecessor. During 1964, the Be-12 established six officially-recognised international altitude records in the FAI class C.3 Group II for turboprop-powered amphibians. These records included an altitude of 39,977 ft. without payload, an altitude of 37,290 ft. with payloads of 2,205 and 4,409 lb., an altitude of 30,682 ft. with a 22,046-lb. payload, and a maximum payload of 22,266 lb. lifted to an altitude of 6,560 ft. On April 24, 1968, a Be-12 established a C.3 Group II 310·6-mile closed-circuit speed record of 343 m.p.h., and two days later established a similar record in C.2 Group II of 351 m.p.h. The largest amphibian flying boat currently in service, the Be-12 is of conventional appearance with a magnetic anomaly detection extension protruding from the rear fuselage, a glazed observation position in the nose, and a fully retractable undercarriage.

BERIEV BE-12 (MAIL)

Estimated Dimensions: Span, 108 ft. 0 in.; length, 96 ft. 0 in.; height, 23 ft. 0 in.

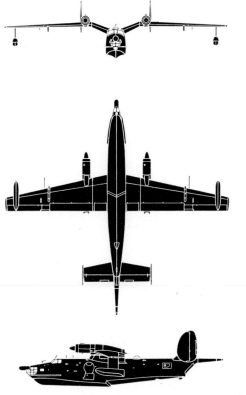

BERIEV BE-30 (CUFF)

Country of Origin: U.S.S.R.
Type: Light Commercial Feederliner.
Power Plants: Two TVD-10 (Turboméca Astazou) turboprops each rated at 970 e.s.h.p.
Performance: (Estimated) Maximum cruising speed, 286 m.p.h. at 6,500 ft.; range (maximum payload—2,860 lb.), 350 mls., (maximum fuel and 1,500-lb. payload), 810 mls.
Weights: Normal loaded, 12,566 lb.
Accommodation: Flight crew of two with normal seating for 15 passengers and alternative high-density arrangement for maximum of 20 passengers.
Status: First prototype flown (with piston engines) March 3, 1967, and second prototype flown (with turboprops) on July 18, 1968. Series production deliveries scheduled to commence 1969.
Notes: Designed specifically for use by Aeroflot as a local-service airliner, the Be-30 has been developed by the G. M. Beriev design bureau in close collaboration with that of Oleg K. Antonov, and initial flight trials with the first prototype were conducted with 740 h.p. ASh-21 air-cooled radial engines. The second prototype is powered by the Astazou XII, but production aircraft are powered by a licence-manufactured version of the Astazou XIV designated TVD-10. The two turboprops are interconnected so that, in the event of the failure of one power plant, the remaining operational engine drives both airscrews.

34

BERIEV BE-30 (CUFF)

Dimensions: Span, 55 ft. 9¼ in.; length, 50 ft. 10¼ in.; height, 18 ft. 3¼ in.; wing area, 344·445 sq. ft.

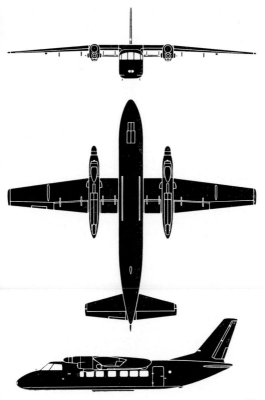

BOEING MODEL 727-200

Country of Origin: U.S.A.

Type: Short- and Medium-range Commercial Transport.

Power Plants: Three Pratt & Whitney JT8D-9 turbofans each rated at 14,500 lb.s.t.

Performance: Maximum speed (at 169,000 lb.), 630 m.p.h. at 22,000 ft.; maximum cruising speed, 592 m.p.h. at 18,000 ft.; economical cruising speed, 553 m.p.h. at 30,000 ft.; range (with maximum payload—42,275 lb.), 1,130 mls., (maximum fuel and 25,000-lb. payload), 2,300 mls.

Weights: Operational empty, 93,725 lb.; maximum loaded, 169,000 lb.

Accommodation: Alternative arrangements available for 179 passengers in high-density configuration, 180 tourist-class passengers, 163 tourist-class passengers, or 14 first-class and 130 tourist-class passengers.

Status: In production. First Model 727-200 flown July 27, 1967, obtaining FAA certification four months later, on November 30, and first delivery (to Northeast) was effected December 11, 1967. The 500th Model 727 (a 727-200 for National) was delivered on December 26, 1967, and approximately 670 Model 727s had been delivered by the beginning of 1969.

Notes: The Model 727-200 is a "stretched" development of the basic Model 727-100 (see 1966 edition) to meet the requirements of the high-density commuter-type market, and differs primarily in having two 10-ft. fuselage sections added, one forward and the other aft of the wing. The Models 727-100C and -100QC are convertible cargo-passenger versions of the short-body Model 727.

36

BOEING MODEL 727-200

Dimensions: Span, 108 ft. 0 in.; length, 153 ft. 2 in.; height, 34 ft. 0 in.; wing area, 1,700 sq. ft.

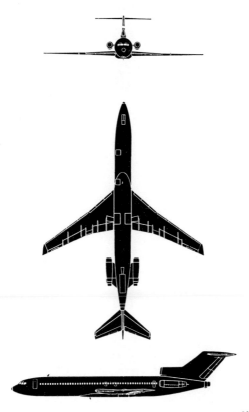

BOEING MODEL 737-200

Country of Origin: U.S.A.

Type: Short-haul Commercial Transport.

Power Plants: Two Pratt & Whitney JT8D-9 turbo-fans each rated at 14,500 lb.s.t.

Performance: Maximum cruising speed, 573 m.p.h. at 26,000 ft.; typical cruising speed, 506 m.p.h. at 30,000 ft.; range (with maximum payload—31,931 lb.), 2,c80 mls.; initial climb rate, 3,200 ft./min.

Weights: Operational empty, 59,225 lb.; maximum loaded, 111,000 lb.

Accommodation: Flight crew of two and alternative arrangements for 88 passengers in five-abreast seating, 91 passengers in mixed-class (28 passengers four abreast and 63 passengers six abreast) seating, or 113 passengers in six-abreast seating.

Status: In production. First Model 737-100 flown on April 9, 1967, followed by the first Model 737-200 flown August 8, 1967. First delivery of 737-100 (to Lufthansa) effected in December 1967, and first delivery of 737-200 (to United Airlines) December 29, 1967. Approximately 110 Model 737s delivered by beginning of 1969, when orders exceeded 230.

Notes: A "long-body" derivative of the Model 737-100 (illustrated above), the Model 737-200 introduced a 6-ft. increase in overall fuselage length, and is also offered in 737-200C and 737-200QC convertible passenger/freighter versions.

38

BOEING MODEL 737-200

Dimensions: Span, 93 ft. 0 in.; length, 100 ft. 0 in.; height, 37 ft. 0 in.; wing area, 980 sq. ft.

BOEING MODEL 747

Country of Origin: U.S.A.

Type: Long-haul Large-capacity Commercial Transport.

Power Plants: Four Pratt & Whitney JT9D-3 turbofans each rated at 43,500 lb.s.t.

Performance: (Estimated) Maximum cruising speed, 615 m.p.h. at 25,000 ft. (Mach 0·89); range cruising speed, 575 m.p.h. at 35,000 ft.; range (with 123,000-lb. payload and normal reserves), 4,600 mls. at range cruising speed; maximum range, 7,080 mls. with 40,000-lb. payload; service ceiling, 40,000 ft.

Weights: Empty, 327,000 lb.; maximum loaded, 710,000 lb.

Accommodation: Flight crew of three–four and alternative interior arrangements for 58 first-class passengers and 308 or 336 economy-class passengers in nine- and ten-abreast seating respectively, and economy-class layouts for 446 or 490 passengers.

Status: In production. First Model 747 was rolled out on September 30, 1968, and was scheduled to fly in January 1969, with first delivery (to Pan American) in September 1969. Orders from 26 airlines totalled 161 aircraft by January 1969. Production of 200 planned by December 1972.

Notes: Mixed-traffic (Model 747C) and all-cargo (Model 747F) versions offered with hinged-nose to permit straight-in freight loading.

BOEING MODEL 747

Dimensions: Span, 195 ft. 8 in.; length, 231 ft. 4 in.;
height, 63 ft. 5 in.; wing area, 5,685 sq. ft.

BREGUET 1150 ATLANTIC

Country of Origin: France.
Type: Long-range Maritime Patrol Aircraft.
Power Plants: Two Hispano-Suiza-built Rolls-Royce
Tyne R.Ty.20 Mk. 21 turboprops each rated at 6,105
e.h.p.
Performance: Maximum speed, 363 m.p.h. at 19,685 ft.;
maximum cruising speed, 342 m.p.h. at 26,250 ft.;
long-range cruising speed (at 95,900 lb.), 311 m.p.h. at
26,250 ft.; maximum endurance cruising speed, 199
m.p.h. below 1,000 ft.; loiter endurance (to and from
patrol area at 311 m.p.h.), 12 hr. at 195 m.p.h. at range
of 620 mls.; ferry range (standard maximum internal
fuel), 4,150 mls.; initial climb rate, 2,450 ft./min.;
service ceiling, 32,800 ft.; maximum endurance, 18 hr.
Weight: Normal loaded, 95,900 lb.
Armament: Internal weapons bay accommodates Mk.
43 Brush or L.K.4 homing torpedoes, all N.A.T.O.
standard bombs, or 386-lb. U.S. or French depth
charges.
Accommodation: Crew of twelve, seven of these being
accommodated in the central operations compartment.
Status: In production. First of three prototypes flown
on October 21, 1961. First production aircraft flown
on July 19, 1965. Total orders for 87 aircraft for
France (40), Germany (20), Netherlands (9), and Italy
(18). Additional orders anticipated from French and
Dutch governments.
Notes: Manufactured by consortium of French,
German, Belgian and Dutch companies. Atlantic
entered service in 1966 with Federal Germany's
Marinefliegergeschwader 3 and France's *Flottille* 21F.

BREGUET 1150 ATLANTIC

Dimensions: Span, 119 ft. 1¼ in.; length, 104 ft. 1½ in.; height, 37 ft. 1¾ in.; wing area, 1,291·67 sq. ft.

BRITTEN–NORMAN BN-2S ISLANDER

Country of Origin: United Kingdom.

Type: Light Utility Transport.

Power Plants: Two Rolls-Royce Continental TSIO-520-E six-cylinder horizontally-opposed engines each rated at 300 h.p.

Performance: Maximum cruising speed (75% power), 180 m.p.h. at 16,000 ft.; economical cruising speed (67% power), 170 m.p.h. at 16,000 ft.; initial climb rate, 1,300 ft./min.

Weights: Maximum loaded, 6,000 lb.

Accommodation: Cabin can accommodate nine passengers in high-density configuration, and several alternative arrangements are available for freighter, ambulance and corporate executive versions, the last-mentioned having a six-seat interior.

Status: Prototype BN-2S flown mid-1968, with production deliveries scheduled May 1969. Prototype BN-2 flown June 12, 1965, with first production BN-2 following August 20, 1966. First production delivery August 1967, and 63 BN-2s were scheduled to have been completed by beginning of 1969 during the course of which year a production rate of one per day is expected to be attained.

Notes: BN-2S is turbo-supercharged development of BN-2A (see 1968 edition). A stretched 12-passenger model with 400 h.p. Lycoming IO-720s and 30-in. additional fuselage section ahead of wing is under test.

44

BRITTEN–NORMAN BN-2S ISLANDER

Dimensions: Span, 49 ft. 0 in.; length, 35 ft. 7¾ in.; height, 12 ft. 4¾ in.; wing area, 325 sq. ft.

CANADAIR CF-5A

Country of Origin: Canada (under U.S. licence).
Type: Single-seat Strike and Reconnaissance Fighter.
Power Plants: Two Orenda J85-Can-15 turbojets each rated at 2,920 lb.s.t. and 4,300 lb.s.t. with afterburning.
Performance: Maximum speed (at 11,630 lb.), 790 m.p.h. (Mach 1·04) at sea level, 977 m.p.h. (Mach 1·48) at 36,000 ft.; long-range cruising speed (maximum external fuel), 560 m.p.h. (Mach 0·85) at 36,000 ft.; tactical radius (hi-lo-hi interdiction mission profile with 1,500-lb. bombs plus two 41·6 and two 125 Imp. gal. external fuel tanks), 575 mls.; ferry range (two 41·6 and three 125 Imp. gal. external tanks), 1,580 mls.; initial climb rate (without external stores), 33,000 ft./min.; combat ceiling, 48,000 ft.
Weights: Empty, 8,681 lb.; empty equipped, 10,380 lb.; loaded (clean), 14,150 lb.; maximum, 20,390 lb.
Armament: Two 20-mm. M-39 cannon with 280 r.p.g., and maximum external ordnance load of 6,200 lb.
Status: In production. First CF-5A flown May 3, 1968, and first CF-5D on August 27, 1968. Eighty-nine single-seat CF-5As and 26 CF-5D two-seaters ordered by Canadian Armed Forces.
Notes: CF-5A is improved version of Northrop F-5A (see 1968 edition) with uprated engines, louvred engine air intake doors, adjustable nosewheel leg, provision for aerial refuelling, additional armour, more extensive avionics, and interchangeable camera nose (illustrated on opposite page). Joint manufacturing programme with Netherlands under which R. Neth. A.F. will receive 73 single-seaters (NF-5A) and 29 two-seaters (NF-5B).

46

CANADAIR CF-5A

Dimensions: Span, 25 ft. 9 in.; length (over probe), 47 ft. 2⅓ in.; height, 13 ft. 2 in.; wing area, 173·82 sq. ft.

CANADAIR CL-215

Country of Origin: Canada.
Type: Air Tanker Utility Transport Amphibious Flying Boat.
Power Plants: Two Pratt & Whitney R-2800-CB-17 radial air-cooled engines each rated at 2,200 b.h.p. (dry) and 2,500 b.h.p. with water injection.
Performance: Maximum cruising speed (at 39,000 lb.), 196 m.p.h. at 10,000 ft., (at 43,000 lb.), 184 m.p.h. at 5,000 ft.; range (with 9,800-lb. payload and 45 min. reserves), 330 mls. or (with 6,000-lb. payload and 45 min. reserves), 1,000 mls. at long-range cruise at 10,000 ft.; initial climb rate (at 43,500 lb.), 1,150 ft./min., (at 40,000 lb.), 1,330 ft./min.
Weights: Operational empty (tanker) 28,040 lb., (freighter), 28,185 lb., (passenger), 30,200 lb.; maximum loaded (tanker), 43,500 lb., (freight-passenger), 40,000 lb.
Accommodation: Flight crew of two and (tanker) two 600 Imp. gal. water tanks plus up to 15 folding passenger seats, or (transport) maximum of 35 passengers.
Status: In production. First of two prototypes flown October 23, 1967. First production aircraft flown September 1968, and first deliveries (to France's *Protection Civile*) scheduled for March 1969. Initial orders for 20 from Quebec Forestry Department and 10 for *Protection Civile*.
Notes: Initially designed specifically for the water bombing of forest fires, the CL-215 is now being offered for a variety of roles, and the latest version (described) differs in several respects from initial production model (2,100 h.p. R-2800-83AM2 engines).

48

CANADAIR CL-215

Dimensions: Span, 93 ft. 10 in.; length, 65 ft. 0¼ in.; height, 29 ft. 3 in.; wing area, 1,080 sq. ft.

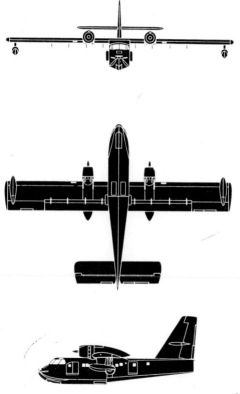

CAVALIER TURBO MUSTANG III

Country of Origin: U.S.A.

Type: Two-seat Close-support Fighter.

Power Plant: One Rolls-Royce Dart (Prototype) Mk. 510 turboprop rated at 1,670 e.h.p., or (Production) Mk. 529 turboprop rated at 2,100 e.h.p.

Performance: (Dart 529) Maximum speed (at 9,450 lb. without external load), 541 m.p.h. at 20,000 ft.; cruising speed, 380 m.p.h. at 20,000 ft., (with two 91·5 Imp. gal. drop tanks and four 250-lb. Mk. 81 low-drag bombs), 345 m.p.h. at 20,000 ft.; long-range cruising speed (with four drop tanks), 326 m.p.h. at 25,000 ft.; tactical radius (with 4,550 lb. ordnance, 15 min. loiter, 10 min. combat and 10% reserves), 576 mls.; ferry range (with 20 min. reserves), 2,300 mls.

Weights: Empty, 6,816 lb.; empty equipped, 8,959 lb.; maximum loaded, 14,000 lb.

Armament: Six M2 or M3 0·5-in. machine guns in wings with 2,000 rounds and up to 5,000 lb. of ordnance on six external pylons.

Status: Experimental. First prototype flown mid-1968.

Notes: Derived from the piston-engined North American P-51D Mustang of W.W.II, the Turbo Mustang III has been evolved by Cavalier Aircraft which specialises in the re-manufacture of P-51Ds as Mustang Is and IIs. The company-funded prototypes, the second of which has full dual control, have Dart Mk. 510 turboprops with Viscount-type cowling, but the proposed production model (from existing or new airframes) will have a Dart Mk. 529 with a cowling of plastic armour, and, in single-seat form, an LW-3B ejector seat.

CAVALIER TURBO MUSTANG III

Dimensions: Span (over tip tanks), 40 ft. 1½ in.; length, 33 ft. 3 in.

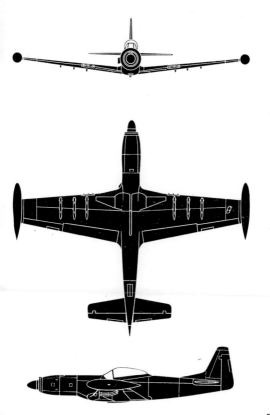

CESSNA FANJET 500

Country of Origin: U.S.A.

Type: Light Executive Transport.

Power Plants: Two Pratt & Whitney JT15D-1 turbo-fans each rated at 2,200 lb.s.t.

Performance: (Estimated) Maximum speed, 413 m.p.h. at 30,000 ft.; maximum cruising speed, 402 m.p.h. at 29,000 ft.; range (with maximum payload), 845 mls. at 35,000 ft. at economical cruise, (with four persons and 160 lb. baggage), 1,330 mls.; initial climb rate, 3,400 ft./min.; service ceiling, 39,000 ft.

Weights: Empty, 5,290 lb.; maximum loaded, 9,500 lb.

Accommodation: Normal flight crew of two, and alternative arrangements for from four to six passengers, the six-passenger arrangement providing for one rearward-facing seat against flight deck bulkhead, two rearward- or forward-facing seats in cabin centre, and a three-place bench seat at cabin rear.

Status: First example scheduled to fly mid-September 1969 with first production units completed last quarter of 1971. First deliveries are scheduled for January 1972 with production tempo attaining eight per month by end of that year.

Notes: Expected to be the lowest-priced business jet available when deliveries commence in 1972, the Fanjet 500 places emphasis on ability to operate from small fields, and on flexibility of cruising altitude to suit the stage length involved.

CESSNA FANJET 500

Dimensions: Span, 44 ft. 0 in.; length, 43 ft. 0 in.; height, 13 ft. 0 in.; wing area, 260 sq. ft.

CESSNA A-37B

Country of Origin: U.S.A.

Type: Two-seat Light Strike and Counter-Insurgency Aircraft.

Power Plants: Two General Electric J85-GE-17A turbojets each rated at 2,850 lb.s.t.

Performance: Maximum speed (without external, stores), 478 m.p.h. at sea level, 507 m.p.h. at 16,000 ft., (with full external stores), 436 m.p.h. at sea level; initial climb rate (at 12,000 lb.), 6,990 ft./min., (at 8,000 lb.), 10,000 ft./min.; combat radius (pilot only, 12,000 lb. gross weight, cruising at 25,000 ft. with 10 min. single-engine loiter at 15,000 ft. and 5 min. combat at sea level), 85 mls. with 4,700 lb. ordnance, 250 mls. with 3,700 lb. ordnance, and 550 mls. with 1,300 lb. ordnance; service ceiling 41,765 ft.; maximum range, 1,012 mls.

Weights: Empty, 5,843 lb.; maximum loaded, 14,000 lb.

Armament: One 7·62-mm. Minigun in fuselage nose and maximum of 5,680 lb. of ordnance on underwing pylons (pilot only).

Status: In production. Thirty-nine A-37As delivered May–September 1967, followed by first A-37Bs from May 1968. Contracts for 228 A-37Bs for 1968–70 delivery placed by September 11, 1968.

Notes: The A-37A is modified from airframe of T-37B trainer and has 2,400 lb.s.t. engines. The A-37B, manufactured for the strike role from the outset, has uprated engines and provision for in-flight refuelling.

54

CESSNA A-37B

Dimensions: Span (over tip-tanks), 35 ft. 10½ in.; length, (over refuelling probe), 31 ft. 4 in.; height, 9 ft. 2 in.; wing area, 183·9 sq. ft.

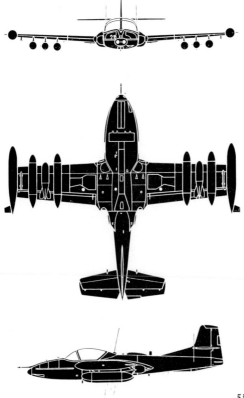

DASSAULT FAN JET FALCON 70

Country of Origin: France.
Type: Light Executive Transport.
Power Plants: Two General Electric CF700-2D turbofans each rated at 4,250 lb.s.t.
Performance: Maximum cruising speed, 535 m.p.h. at 25,000 ft.; economical cruising speed, 466 m.p.h. at 40,000 ft.; range (with maximum fuel, a 1,600-lb. payload and 45 min. reserves), 1,870 mls. at econ. cruise, or 1,400 mls. at 520 m.p.h. at 25,000 ft.; service ceiling, 42,000 ft.
Weights: Empty equipped, 15,840 lb.; maximum loaded, 28,660 lb.
Accommodation: Crew of two and normal seating for eight passengers in individual seats. Alternative arrangements for 10–14 passengers.
Status: (Model 68) In production. Prototype flown on May 4, 1963, and first production example on January 1, 1965, with 100th delivered on July 20, 1967. Current Model 68 to be supplanted in production by Model 70 during 1969 for 1970 delivery.
Notes: Model 70 differs from Model 68 in having increased internal fuel capacity (from 1,047 Imp. gal. to 1,134 Imp. gal.); a new high-lift system for the wing, reducing balanced field take-off and landing distances from 6,200 to 5,500 ft. and 3,900 to 3,500 ft. respectively, and a 1,324 lb. increase in maximum take-off weight. The 5,000 lb.s.t. Garrett-AiResearch ATF-3 engine may later be installed. A Model 68 of the Canadian Armed Forces is illustrated above, and Pan America's Business Jets Division has ordered 20 and taken options on a further 80 of the Model 70.

56

DASSAULT FAN JET FALCON 70

Dimensions: Span, 53 ft. 6 in.; length, 56 ft. 3 in.; height, 17 ft. 5 in.; wing area, 440 sq. ft.

DASSAULT MD.320 HIRONDELLE

Country of Origin: France.
Type: Light Utility Transport.
Power Plants: Two Turboméca Astazou XIV turbo-props each rated at 858 b.h.p.
Performance: Maximum cruising speed (at 11,750 lb.), 311 m.p.h.; long-range cruising speed (at 12,235 lb.), 249 m.p.h.; range (with 6–8 passengers and 45 min. reserves), 1,926 mls., (with 10–12 passengers), 1,240 mls.; service ceiling, 29,530 ft.
Weights: Empty equipped (freighter), 7,100 lb.; (12-passenger version), 7,430 lb.; maximum loaded, 12,235 lb.
Accommodation: Flight crew of two and eight, 10, or 12 passengers in alternative feederliner arrangements, or six passengers in executive version.
Status: Prototype flown on September 11, 1968.
Notes: The Hirondelle has been designed with a view to both commercial and military application, and is currently being offered to the *Armée de l'Air* for the liaison, utility transport and navigational training roles. A further development of the basic design powered by two SNECMA/Turboméca M-49 Larzac turbofans of 2,290 lb.s.t. is proposed for 1972–73. More immediate application is foreseen of the Astazou XVI of 986 b.h.p. with which the Hirondelle is expected to attain a maximum cruising speed of 354 m.p.h.

DASSAULT MD.320 HIRONDELLE

Dimensions: Span, 47 ft. 8¾ in.; length, 40 ft. 2¼ in.; wing area, 290·62 sq. ft.

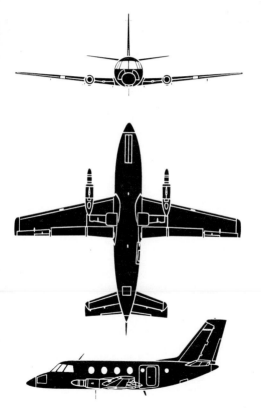

DASSAULT MIRAGE F1

Country of Origin: France.

Type: Single-seat Interceptor and Strike Fighter.

Power Plant: One SNECMA Atar 9K-50 turbojet rated at 11,067 lb.s.t. and 15,784 lb.s.t. with afterburning.

Performance: Maximum speed, 1,450 m.p.h. at 40,000 ft. (Mach 2·2), 835 m.p.h. at sea level (Mach 1·1); maximum endurance, 3·75 hr.; service ceiling, 65,000 ft.; range (with maximum external fuel), 2,050 mls.

Weights: Empty, 16,425 lb.; loaded, 24,470 lb.; maximum, 32,630 lb.

Armament: (Intercept) Two 30-mm. DEFA cannon, two MATRA R.530 and two AIM-9 Sidewinder AAMs, (attack) maximum of 14 250-lb. bombs on seven external pylons, or mixed conventional ordnance including two Nord AS.30 ASMs.

Status: Development. First prototype flown December 23, 1966, and destroyed May 18, 1967. Three pre-production aircraft ordered May 26, 1967, and first (illustrated above) was scheduled to fly February 1969. Production of initial batch of 30 to commence second half of 1969, with deliveries to *Armée de l'Air* 1970–71.

Notes: Evolved from the Mirage IIIE (see 1967 edition) and using some of the systems and much of the fuselage structure of this aircraft, the Mirage F1 has swept wing, conventional tail, uprated engine, CSF head-up display equipment, and CSF Cyrano IV radar including both air-to-air and air-to-ground modes. Variants of the Mirage envisaged include the less sophisticated export F1A, the tandem two-seat F1B, and the J79-J1Q-powered F1C. The Mirage F1 can operate within a 2,600-ft field length at average combat weight.

60

DASSAULT MIRAGE F1

Dimensions: Span, 29 ft. 10⅗ in.; length, 49 ft. 2½ in.;
height, 14 ft. 9 in.

DASSAULT MIRAGE G

Country of Origin: France.
Type: Two-seat Strike and Reconnaissance Fighter.
Power Plant: One SNECMA TF-306E turbofan rated
at 11,684 lb.s.t. and 20,503 lb.s.t. with afterburning.
Performance: (Estimated) Maximum speed, 840 m.p.h.
at sea level (Mach 1·1), 1,650 m.p.h. at 40,000 ft.
(Mach 2·5); initial climb rate, 35,000 ft./min.; en-
durance (maximum external fuel at economical cruise),
8 hr.; service ceiling, 65,000 ft.; ferry range, 4,000 mls.
Weights: Empty, 22,500 lb.; loaded, 33,500 lb.
Armament: (Mirage G4) Conventional or nuclear
stores on six external stations, and two 30-mm.
cannon internally.
Status: Experimental. First prototype flown October
18, 1967. Two prototypes of twin-engined derivative
(Mirage G4) ordered September 1968, with first
scheduled to fly by 1971.
Notes: Essentially a variable-geometry equivalent of
the Mirage F2 (see 1967 edition), the Mirage G is
currently under development to provide a strike and
reconnaissance fighter for *Armée de l'Air* use from
1975. The Mirage G's wing is swept 20° when fully
extended and 70° in the full aft position, and translates
from full forward to full aft in approximately 20
seconds. Mirage G4 derivative will be powered by
two Atar 9K-53 turbojets, will be larger than the current prototype, and will have a maximum loaded
weight of the order of 60,000 lb., single-seat high-
altitude intercept and two-seat attack versions being
proposed.

DASSAULT MIRAGE G

Dimensions: Span (maximum sweep), 22 ft. 11½ in.,
(minimum sweep), 49 ft. 2½ in.; length, 55 ft. 1½ in.;
height, 17 ft. 6½ in.

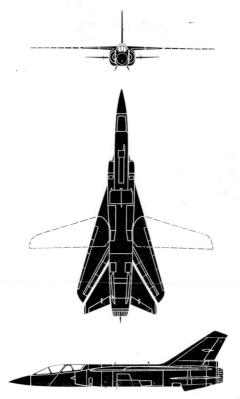

DASSAULT MIRAGE M5

Country of Origin: France.

Type: Single-seat Tactical Fighter-Bomber.

Power Plant: One SNECMA Atar 9C turbojet rated at 9,436 lb.s.t. and 13,624 lb.s.t. with afterburning.

Performance: Maximum speed, 875 m.p.h. at sea level (Mach 1·15), 1,386 m.p.h. at 40,000 ft. (Mach 2·1); range cruising speed, 594 m.p.h. at 36,000 ft. (Mach 0·9); endurance (maximum external fuel), 4 hr.

Weights: Empty equipped, 14,550 lb.; maximum loaded, 29,760 lb.

Armament: Two 30-mm. DEFA 5-52 cannon plus more than 8,800 lb. external ordnance. Typical load for short-range interdiction mission comprises two 1,000-lb., ten 500-lb. and two 250-lb. bombs, plus two 110 Imp. gal. auxiliary fuel tanks.

Status: In production. Deliveries initiated (to Peru) mid-1968.

Notes: The Mirage M5 is an export version of the Mirage IIIE (see 1967 edition) optimised for the ground attack role and featuring simplified avionics. Fifty ordered by Israel (Mirage 5-J) and completed mid-1968, but embargo placed by French government on delivery. Twelve (Mirage 5-P illustrated above) delivered to Peru and 88 ordered by Belgium of which 54 (Mirage 5-BA) for ground attack, 22 (Mirage 5-BR) for tactical reconnaissance, and 12 as two-seaters (Mirage 5-BD) for training. Claimed to be the lowest-priced combat aircraft possessing Mach 2·0 capability, the Mirage M5 differs from the IIIE only in having the fire control radar, Doppler and TACAN deleted and facilities for the rocket motor removed.

DASSAULT MIRAGE M5

Dimensions: Span, 26 ft. $11\frac{1}{2}$ in.; length, 51 ft. $0\frac{1}{4}$ in.; height, 13 ft. $11\frac{1}{2}$ in.; wing area, 375·12 sq. ft.

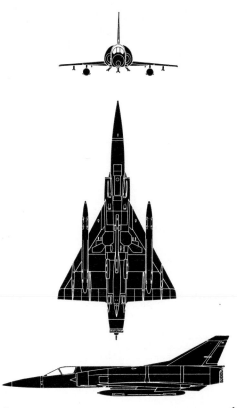

DE HAVILLAND CANADA DHC-5 BUFFALO

Country of Origin: Canada.

Type: Military Tactical and Utility Transport.

Power Plants: Two General Electric T64-GE-14 turboprops each rated at 3,060 e.s.h.p.

Performance: Maximum speed, 282 m.p.h. at 10,000 ft.; cruising speed at 80% power, 253 m.p.h., at 52% power, 208 m.p.h.; initial climb rate, 2,080 ft./min.; service ceiling, 31,500 ft.; range (with maximum payload—12,780 lb.), 553 mls., (with 8,000-lb. payload), 1,300 mls., (with 4,000-lb. payload), 1,958 mls., (maximum fuel, no payload), 2,142 mls.

Weights: Operational empty, 24,220 lb.; maximum loaded, 41,000 lb.

Accommodation: Crew of three plus 41 troops, 35 paratroops, or 24 casualty stretchers.

Status: In production. First of four evaluation aircraft (CV-7) flown April 9, 1964. Deliveries against initial order for 15 (CC-115) for Canadian Armed Forces' Mobile Command commenced 1967 and scheduled for completion by beginning of 1969. Twelve ordered for Brazilian Air Force delivered 1968, and second batch of 12 ordered for 1969 delivery.

Notes: Originally designed primarily to meet a U.S. Army requirement. Four delivered to this service of which three survivors transferred in 1967 to NASA when U.S.A.F. assumed responsibility for fixed-wing intra-theatre airlift. A commercial version, the DHC-5C, is offered with accommodation for 47–53 passengers.

DE HAVILLAND CANADA DHC-5 BUFFALO

Dimensions: Span, 96 ft. 0 in.; length, 79 ft. 0 in.;
height, 28 ft. 8 in.; wing area, 945 sq. ft.

DE HAVILLAND CANADA DHC-6
TWIN OTTER SRS. 200

Country of Origin: Canada.
Type: Light STOL Utility Transport and Feederliner.
Power Plants: Two Pratt & Whitney PT6A-20A turbo-props each rated at 579 e.s.h.p.
Performance: Maximum cruising speed, 190 m.p.h. at 10,000 ft.; cruising speed (80% max. continuous power), 172 m.p.h.; range cruising speed, 155 m.p.h.; initial climb rate, 1,300 ft./min.; service ceiling, 24,300 ft.; range with 30 min. reserves at 155 m.p.h. (maximum payload—4,296 lb.), 100 mls., (maximum fuel and 2,420-lb. payload), 945 mls.
Weights: Empty, 5,850 lb.; empty equipped (13-seat utility version), 6,050 lb.; maximum loaded, 11,579 lb.
Accommodation: Side-by-side seats for two crew members. Cabin accommodates 13–18 passengers with 88 cu. ft. baggage compartment.
Status: In production. First of five pre-production (Srs.100) aircraft flown May 20, 1965. Approximately 180 completed by beginning of 1969 when production rate was being raised to nine per month.
Notes: Series 200, introduced April 1968, differs from Series 100 (see 1968 edition), which it succeeded, in having increased baggage capacity and a lengthened nose. The Series 300, which is scheduled to be delivered from May 1969, differs from the Series 200 in having 640 e.s.h.p. PT6A-27 turboprops and a 12,500-lb. loaded weight.
68

DE HAVILLAND CANADA DHC-6
TWIN OTTER SRS. 200

Dimensions: Span, 65 ft. 0 in.; length, 51 ft. 8½ in.;
height, 18 ft. 7 in.; wing area, 420 sq. ft.

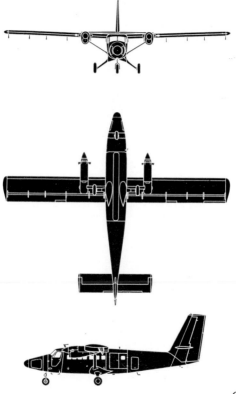

DORNIER D-2 SKYSERVANT

Country of Origin: Federal Germany.
Type: Light STOL Freighter and Feederliner.
Power Plants: Two Lycoming IGSO-540-A1E six-cylinder horizontally-opposed engines each rated at 380 h.p.
Performance: (At 8,050 lb.) Maximum speed, 199 m.p.h. at 10,500 ft.; cruising speed (75% power), 161 m.p.h. at sea level, 169 m.p.h. at 5,000 ft., 177 m.p.h. at 10,000 ft., (65% power), 152 m.p.h. at sea level, 161 m.p.h. at 5,000 ft., 167 m.p.h. at 10,000 ft.; maximum range, 1,143 mls. at 143 m.p.h. at 10,000 ft.; initial climb rate, 1,180 ft./min.; service ceiling, 24,300 ft.
Weights: Empty, 4,620 lb.; max. loaded, 8,050 lb.
Accommodation: Pilot and 8–14 passengers.
Status: In production. First of three prototypes flown February 23, 1966, and first production deliveries effected late 1967, an output of four per month being attained by mid-1968. Production rate scheduled to be raised to 6–8 per month early 1969.
Notes: Capable of operation from skis and floats, the Skyservant places accent on ease of maintenance and 125 are to be delivered to the *Luftwaffe* and German Army with deliveries scheduled for completion in 1972.

DORNIER D-2 SKYSERVANT

Dimensions: Span, 50 ft. 10¾ in.; length, 37 ft. 4¾ in.;
height, 12 ft. 9½ in.; wing area, 308 sq. ft.

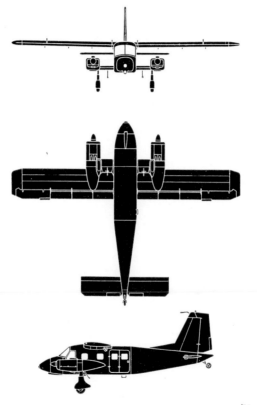

DOUGLAS A-4F SKYHAWK

Country of Origin: U.S.A.

Type: Single-seat Shipboard Attack Bomber.

Power Plant: One Pratt & Whitney J52-P-8A turbojet rated at 9,300 lb.s.t.

Performance: Maximum speed (without external stores), 675 m.p.h. at sea level (Mach 0·88), 612 m.p.h. at 35,000 ft. (Mach 0·92); maximum speed in high drag configuration, 610 m.p.h. at sea level (Mach 0·8), 575 m.p.h. at 30,000 ft. (Mach 0·85); combat radius (with 4,000 lb. external stores), 380 mls.; ferry range (max. fuel), 2,440 mls.; service ceiling (clean), 47,900 ft.

Weights: Empty, 9,940 lb.; loaded (clean), 16,300 lb.; maximum loaded, 27,420 lb.

Armament: Two 20-mm. Mk. 12 cannon with 100 r.p.g. plus a maximum of 8,200 lb. of stores for shipboard and 11,800 lb. for shore-based operation.

Status: In production. First A-4F flown August 31, 1966. Deliveries of 150 initiated June 20, 1967.

Notes: A-4F differs from A-4E in having more powerful engine, steerable nosewheel, zero-zero escape system, avionics compartment aft of cockpit and wing, lift spoilers. Tandem two-seat training version, the TA-4F, also being manufactured with 139 on order. Export equivalents comprise A-4G (8), illustrated above, and TA-4G for Australian Navy; A-4H (65) and TA-4H (8) for Israel, and A-4K (10) and TA-4K (4) for R.N.Z.A.F.

72

DOUGLAS A-4F SKYHAWK

Dimensions: Span, 27 ft. 6 in.; length, 42 ft. 10¾ in.;
height, 15 ft. 2 in.; wing area, 260 sq. ft.

DOUGLAS C-9A NIGHTINGALE

Country of Origin: U.S.A.

Type: Aeromedical Evacuation Transport.

Power Plants: Two Pratt & Whitney JT8D-9 turbofans each rated at 14,500 lb.s.t.

Performance: Maximum cruising speed, 565 m.p.h. at 25,000 lb.; long-range cruising speed, 510 m.p.h. at 30,000 ft.; maximum range at long-range cruising speed, 2,800 mls. at 30,000 ft.

Weights: Empty equipped, 59,200 lb.; maximum loaded, 108,000 lb.

Accommodation: Flight crew of three, four–six medical personnel, and 40 ambulatory patients in four-abreast seating, 30 casualty stretchers on three-high tiers, 40 casualty stretchers on four-high tiers, or various combinations of ambulatory and stretcher patients.

Status: In production. First of 12 C-9A transports for the U.S.A.F.'s Military Airlift Command flown June 1968, and first delivery (to the 375th Aeromedical Airlift Wing) effected in August 1968.

Notes: The C-9A Nightingale is basically similar to the commercial DC-9-30 (see 1968 edition) transport, but introduces an 11-ft. wide cargo door and a special ramp to facilitate the loading and unloading of casualty stretchers. The highly-specialised interior of the Nightingale includes an isolated special-care section, refrigerated storage facilities for medical supplies, and a 110-volt, 60-cycle electrical system permitting on-board use of standard hospital medical equipment.

DOUGLAS C-9A NIGHTINGALE

Dimensions: Span, 93 ft. 4¾ in.; length, 119 ft. 3½ in.;
height, 27 ft. 4¾ in.; wing area, 1,000·7 sq. ft.

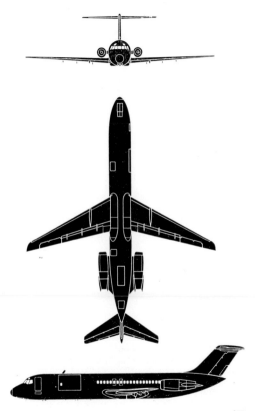

DOUGLAS DC-8 SUPER 60 SERIES

Country of Origin: U.S.A.

Type: Long-range Commercial Transport.

Power Plants: Four Pratt & Whitney JT3D-3B turbofans each rated at 18,000 lb.s.t., or (Super 63) JT3D-7 turbofans each rated at 19,000 lb.s.t.

Performance: (Variant indicated in parentheses) Maximum cruising speed at 220,000 lb., (61) 580 m.p.h., (62) 586 m.p.h., (63) 583 m.p.h.; initial climb rate at max. loaded weight, (61) 2,270 ft./min., (62) 2,240 ft./min., (63) 2,165 ft./min.; max. range without payload, (61) 7,370 mls., (62) 8,780 mls., (63) 8,100 mls.

Weights: Operational empty, (61) 150,298 lb., (62) 143,653 lb., (63) 156,755 lb.; maximum loaded, (61) 325,000 lb., (62) 335,000 lb., (63) 350,000 lb.

Accommodation: The maximum economy class passenger accommodation of the Super 60 series is as follows: (61) 251, (62) 189, (63) 251 plus 14,000 lb. freight. The space-limited payloads of the freighter equivalents are: (61F) 91,250 lb., (62F) 96,754 lb., (63F) 91,614 lb.

Status: In production. First DC-8-61 flown March 14, 1966, first DC-8-62 flown August 29, 1966 and first DC-8-63 flown April 10, 1967.

Notes: Stretched derivatives of DC-8-50 (see 1966 edition). DC-8-61 and -61F feature 36·9-ft. increase in fuselage length. DC-8-62 (illustrated above) and -62F have shorter fuselage, 3-ft. wingtip extensions, new engine pylons suspending the engines 40 in. forward of previous installations, and redesigned long-duct engine pods offering reduced drag. The DC-8-63 (illustrated opposite) and -63F have similar fuselage to -61 coupled with aerodynamic refinements of -62.

76

DOUGLAS DC-8 SUPER 60 SERIES

Dimensions: Span (61), 142 ft. 4¾ in., (62 and 63) 148 ft.
4¾ in.; length (61 and 63), 187 ft. 4¾ in., (62) 157 ft.
4¾ in.; height, 42 ft. 3½ in.; wing area (61), 2,884 sq.
ft., (62 and 63) 2,926·8 sq. ft.

DOUGLAS DC-9 SERIES 20

Country of Origin: U.S.A.

Type: Short- to Medium-range Commercial Transport.

Power Plants: Two Pratt & Whitney JT8D-9 turbofans each rated at 14,500 lb.s.t.

Performance: Maximum cruising speed, 560 m.p.h. at 25,000 ft.; range (with 50 passengers and reserves for 230 miles and 60 min. holding at 10,000 ft.), 1,397 mls. at 25,000 ft., (at long-range cruising speed), 1,840 mls. at 30,000 ft.

Weights: Empty, 51,661 lb.; maximum loaded, 98,000 lb.

Accommodation: Flight crew of two–three, and maximum of 90 tourist-class passengers in five-abreast seating.

Status: In production. First DC-9-20 flown on September 18, 1968, and first deliveries (to S.A.S.) were scheduled for December 1968. More than 400 DC-9s of all versions had been completed by the beginning of 1969.

Notes: Claimed to possess the highest lift coefficient of any commercial transport, and capable of operating from airfields previously accessible only to airscrew-driven aircraft, the DC-9-20 combines the short DC-9-10 (see 1966 edition) fuselage with the wing developed for the larger DC-9-30 (see 1968 edition). A further version with a 21-ft. longer fuselage than that of the DC-9-20 but with similar wings and power plants is the DC-9-40 which was flown for the first time on November 28, 1967.

78

DOUGLAS DC-9 SERIES 20

Dimensions: Span, 93 ft. $3\frac{1}{2}$ in.; length, 104 ft. $4\frac{3}{4}$ in.; height, 27 ft. 6 in.; wing area, 1,000·7 sq. ft.

EFW C-3605

Country of Origin: Switzerland.

Type: Two-seat Target Tug.

Power Plant: One Lycoming T53O7A turboprop rated at 1,150 e.s.h.p.

Performance: Maximum speed, 268 m.p.h. at 10,000 ft.; normal cruising speed, 218 m.p.h.; endurance, 2 hr. 30 min., (with auxiliary underwing tanks), 4 hr. 30 min.; range with 30 min. reserves, 609 mls., (with auxiliary tanks), 995 mls.; initial climb rate, 2,470 ft./min.; service ceiling, 32,810 ft.; time to service ceiling, 22 min.

Weights: Empty, 5,800 lb.; normal loaded, 7,275 lb.; maximum, 8,185 lb.

Status: Prototype conversion flown August 19, 1968. Current proposals for conversion of a further 20 C-3603 airframes to C-3605 standard.

Notes: The C-3605 is a turboprop conversion of the piston-engined C-3603 undertaken by the EFW (Eidgenössisches Flugzeugwerk, or Federal Aircraft Factory) to meet a Swiss Air Force target tug requirement. The conversion is confined to the replacement of the Hispano–Suiza 12Y-51 engine and Escher–Wyss airscrew by a T53O7A driving a Hamilton Standard airscrew, the lower weight of the turboprop having necessitated the introduction of an additional 6-ft. section in the forward fuselage for c.g. reasons. A hydraulic winch replaces the impeller-driven system previously employed by the C-3603. Thirty-seven of the 160 C-3603s built 1941–44 remain airworthy, many with relatively low airframe hours, and most serve as target tugs.

EFW C-3605

Dimensions: Span, 45 ft. 1 in.; length, 40 ft. 8¼ in.;
height, 13 ft. 3½ in.; wing area, 308·92 sq. ft.

FIAT G.91Y

Country of Origin: Italy.
Type: Single-seat Strike and Reconnaissance Fighter.
Power Plant: Two General Electric J85-GE-13A turbojets each rated at 2,725 lb.s.t. and 4,080 lb.s.t. with afterburning.
Performance: Maximum speed, 714 m.p.h. at sea level (Mach 0·94), 690 m.p.h. at 32,810 ft. (Mach 0·975); climb to 19,685 ft., 1·5 min., to 29,530 ft., 2·3 min.; service ceiling, 41,200 ft.; sea level tactical radius, 465 mls.; ferry range, 2,175 mls.
Weights: Empty, 8,378 lb.; normal loaded, 17,196 lb.; maximum loaded, 19,180 lb.
Armament: Four 0·5-in. Colt–Browning machine guns and four 500-lb. bombs, twelve 3-in. HVAR rockets, or two Nord AS.20 or AS.30L ASMs.
Status: In production. First prototype flown December 27, 1966, and second in September 1967. Twenty pre-production examples being followed by 55 production aircraft.
Notes: Although bearing a close resemblance to the Fiat G.91R (see 1966 edition), the G.91Y possesses little commonality with its predecessor which it is intended to replace in Italian Air Force service. While the basic concept remains unchanged, the G.91Y possesses appreciably more power and offers substantially improved load-carrying capability. Like the G.91R, the G.91Y is intended to operate from semi-prepared strips, and a tandem two-seat trainer version, the G.91YT, is currently proposed.

FIAT G.91Y

Dimensions: Span, 29 ft. 6½ in.; length, 38 ft. 3½ in.; height, 14 ft. 6⅓ in.; wing area, 195·149 sq. ft.

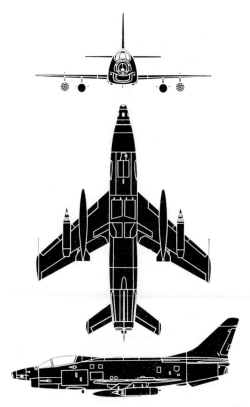

FIAT G.222

Country of Origin: Italy.
Type: Medium-range Tactical Transport.
Power Plants: Two General Electric T64-P4C turbo-props each rated at 3,400 s.h.p.
Performance: (Estimated) Maximum speed, 329 m.p.h. at 55,115 lb. at sea level; long-range cruising speed, 249 m.p.h. at 14,750 ft.; range (with 14,330-lb. pay-load), 1,240 mls., (with maximum fuel and 3,640 lb.), 3,100 mls.; time to 14,750 ft. (at 54,000 lb.), 10 min. 30 sec.; service ceiling, 29,500 ft.
Weights: (Estimated) Empty, 28,000 lb.; normal loaded, 54,000 lb.; maximum loaded, 58,420 lb.
Accommodation: Normal flight crew of three–four, and 44 fully-equipped troops, 40 paratroops, or 36 casualty stretchers.
Status: First of two prototypes scheduled to commence flight test programme late 1969.
Notes: The G.222 is being developed jointly by Fiat and Aerfer to meet an Italian Air Force requirement for a replacement for the service's current Fairchild C-119G and C-119J transports. No production order had been placed at the time of closing for press.
84

FIAT G.222

Dimensions: Span, 94 ft. 2 in.; length, 74 ft. 5½ in.; height, 32 ft. 1¾ in.; wing area, 882·64 sq. ft.

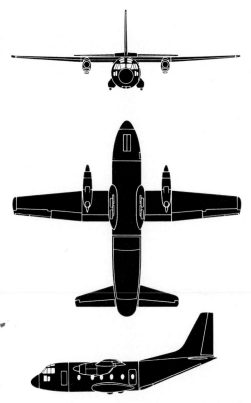

FOKKER F.27 FRIENDSHIP SRS. 500

Country of Origin: Netherlands.
Type: Short- to Medium-range Commercial Transport.
Power Plants: Two Rolls-Royce Dart 532-7 turbo-props each rated at 2,250 e.s.h.p.
Performance: Maximum cruising speed, 322 m.p.h. at 20,000 ft.; long-range cruising speed, 291 m.p.h. at 20,000 ft.; range (maximum fuel, 8,914-lb. payload and reserves), 1,135 mls.; range (with 10,950-lb. payload), 430 mls.; initial climb rate (at 40,000 lb.), 1,450 ft./min.
Weights: Empty, 24,650 lb.; operational empty, 25,380 lb.; maximum loaded, 43,500 lb.
Accommodation: Basic flight crew of two or three, and alternative arrangements for 52 or 56 passengers.
Status: In production. First Friendship 500 flown November 15, 1967. Approximately 270 Friendships of all versions delivered by parent company by beginning of 1969.
Notes: By comparison with the Series 200 (see 1968 edition), the Series 500 has a 4 ft. 11 in. increase in fuselage length resulting from additional sections being inserted fore and aft of the wing. The large cargo door originally featured by the Series 300 and 400 "Combiplane" convertible cargo or combined cargo-and-freighter versions. A basically similar stretched version of the Friendship is manufactured under licence in the U.S.A. by Fairchild Hiller as the FH-227B (see 1968 edition).

FOKKER F.27 FRIENDSHIP SRS. 500

Dimensions: Span, 95 ft. 1¾ in.; length, 82 ft. 2½ in.;
height, 28 ft. 7¼ in.; wing area, 754 sq. ft.

FOKKER F.28 FELLOWSHIP

Country of Origin: Netherlands.

Type: Short-haul Commercial Transport.

Power Plants: Two Rolls-Royce RB.183-2 Mk. 555-15 Spey Junior turbofans each rated at 9,850 lb.s.t.

Performance: Maximum cruising speed, 527 m.p.h. at 21,000 ft.; economical cruising speed, 519 m.p.h. at 25,000 ft.; long-range cruising speed, 426 m.p.h.; range (with 60 passengers and 10% reserves), 1,160 mls. at 30,000 ft.

Weights: Operational empty, 33,800 lb.; maximum loaded, 62,000 lb.

Accommodation: Alternative arrangements for 40 passengers in first-class seating four abreast, or 55, 60 or 65 passengers in five-abreast all-tourist seating.

Status: In production. First of three prototypes flown May 9, 1967, and first production aircraft flown on May 21, 1968. First production deliveries (to L.T.U and Braathens S.A.F.E.) were scheduled for early 1969.

Notes: The F.28 Fellowship is a European co-operative effort in which the nose section is of Fokker design and production; fuselage section 1 is of Fokker design and VFW construction; fuselage sections 2 and 3 are of Fokker design and production; wing centre section is of Fokker design and production; outer wing is of Short Brothers design and production; fuselage section 4 and engine nacelles are of HFB design and construction, and the tail assembly is of VFW design and construction. The F.28 is to be distributed in the U.S.A. by Fairchild Hiller, an initial order for 10 having been placed.

FOKKER F.28 FELLOWSHIP

Dimensions: Span, 77 ft. 4¼ in.; length, 89 ft. 10¾ in.; height, 27 ft. 9½ in.; wing area, 822 sq. ft.

GARDAN GY-100 BAGHEERA

Country of Origin: France.

Type: Light Cabin Monoplane.

Power Plant: One Lycoming O-235-C1B or Lycoming O-320 four-cylinder horizontally-opposed engine rated at 115 h.p. and 135 h.p. respectively.

Performance: (Specification relates to GY-100 with 115 h.p. engine, figures in parentheses relating to version with 135 h.p. engine) Maximum speed, 140 (146) m.p.h. at sea level; cruising speed at 75% power, 124 (126) m.p.h.; range at economical cruise, 497 (528) mls.; service ceiling, 21,750 (22,990) ft.

Weights: Empty, 1,058 (1,091) lb.; maximum loaded, 1,775 (2,021) lb.

Accommodation: Two persons seated side by side with third person seated centrally aft.

Status: First prototype flown December 21, 1967. Initial production series of 35 scheduled for completion by mid-1969.

Notes: The Bagheera, named after the panther of Kipling's "Jungle Book", has been designed by Yves Gardan, designer of the SOCATA Horizon, and is intended to be produced as a two-seater with a 115 h.p. engine, a three-seater with a 135 h.p. engine, and a four-seater with a 200 h.p. engine. The prototype is powered by a 150 h.p. Lycoming O-320 derated to 135 h.p. The Bagheera is of all-metal construction.

GARDAN GY-100 BAGHEERA

Dimensions: Span, 26 ft. 10¾ in.; length, 19 ft. 5¼ in.;
height, 6 ft. 6¾ in.; wing area, 131·32 sq. ft.

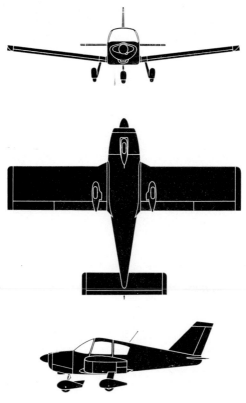

GENERAL DYNAMICS F-111A

Country of Origin: U.S.A.

Type: Two-seat Tactical Strike and Reconnaissance Fighter.

Power Plants: Two Pratt & Whitney TF30-P-3 turbofans each rated at approx. 12,500 lb.s.t. and 21,000 lb.s.t. with afterburning.

Performance: Maximum speed, 1,650 m.p.h. at 40,000 ft. (Mach 2·5), 865 m.p.h. at sea level (Mach 1·2); service ceiling (without external stores), 55,000–60,000 ft., (with maximum conventional bomb load), 30,000–35,000 ft.; tactical radius (hi-lo-hi mission with 16,000-lb. combat load), 1,500–1,700 mls.; ferry range, 3,500–4,000 mls.

Weights: Empty, 42,000 lb.; normal loaded, 81,400 lb.

Armament: One 20-mm. General Electric M-61A1 rotary cannon with 2,000 rounds, and ordnance loads such as 12 750-lb. M.117 bombs on triple ejector racks attached to four swivelling inboard pylons.

Status: In production. First operationally-configured F-111A (31st aircraft) delivered to U.S.A.F. October 1967. Production of 12–13 of all versions of F-111 (including FB-111A) monthly scheduled to be maintained throughout 1969.

Notes: Variants of basic F-111 design include the F-111C for the R.A.A.F. with extended wing and strengthened undercarriage of the FB-111 (see pages 94–5), the first of 24 examples of which flew in July 1968; the F-111D featuring more advanced avionics than those installed in the F-111A, and the RF-111D for reconnaissance with cameras, radar and infra-red sensors.

GENERAL DYNAMICS F-111A

Dimensions: Span, 63 ft. 0 in., (maximum sweep), 31 ft. 11 in.; length, 73 ft. 6 in.; height, 17 ft. 1½ in.

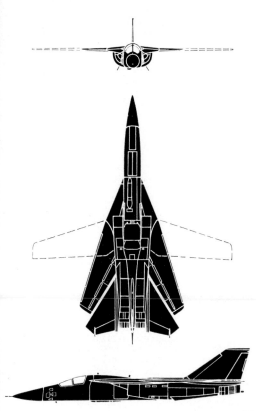

GENERAL DYNAMICS FB-111A

Country of Origin: U.S.A.

Type: Two-seat Strategic Bomber.

Power Plants: Two Pratt & Whitney TF30-P-7 turbofans each rated at approx. 13,000 lb.s.t. and 22,000 lb.s.t. with afterburning.

Performance: (Estimated) Maximum speed (without external stores), 1,450 m.p.h. at 40,000 ft. (Mach 2·2), 838 m.p.h. at sea level (Mach 1·1); normal combat radius, 1,250 mls.; maximum ferry range, 4,100 mls.

Weights: Maximum loaded, 110,000 lb.

Armament: Four Boeing AGM-69A (Short-range Attack Missiles) or conventional ordnance loads up to maximum of 36,000 lb. (e.g. 48 750-lb. bombs on multiple ejection racks on four swivelling and four fixed pylons).

Status: In production. Prototype flown July 30, 1967, and first production aircraft flown July 13, 1968. Initial orders for 64 with deliveries to U.S.A.F. Strategic Air Command commencing 1969.

Notes: An interim strategic bomber derivative of the F-111A tactical strike and reconnaissance fighter (see pages 92–3), the FB-111A features an extended wing, a strengthened undercarriage with increased braking capacity to cater for higher take-off and landing weights, and advanced all-digital computer-controlled avionics for navigation and air-to-ground weapons delivery. The non-swivelling outer pylons are intended for subsonic flight and are jettisoned when wing sweep exceeds 26° for supersonic flight. Planned total of 253 reduced by 163 late 1968.

GENERAL DYNAMICS FB-111A

Dimensions: Span, 70 ft. 0 in., (maximum sweep), 33 ft. 11 in.; length, 73 ft. 6 in.; height, 17 ft. 0 in.

GRUMMAN A-6A INTRUDER

Country of Origin: U.S.A.
Type: Two-seat Shipboard Low-level Strike Aircraft.
Power Plants: Two Pratt & Whitney J52-P-8A turbojets each rated at 9,300 lb.s.t.
Performance: Maximum speed, 685 m.p.h. at sea level (Mach 0·9), 625 m.p.h. at 36,000 ft. (Mach 0·95); normal cruising speed, 480 m.p.h. at 28,000 ft.; low-level long-range cruising speed (high drag configuration), 345 m.p.h.; range at low-altitude (internal fuel only), 1,250 mls., (with five 250 Imp. gal./300 U.S. gal. drop tanks), 1,950 mls.; ferry range, 3,225 mls. at 28,000 ft.
Weights: Empty, 25,684 lb.; loaded (maximum internal fuel), 43,000 lb.; max. overload, 60,626 lb.
Armament: Maximum offensive load for limited-range interdiction is 15,000 lb. distributed on five 3,600-lb. capacity pylons. Typical conventional loads include eighteen 500-lb. Mk. 82 bombs plus two 250 Imp. gal./300 U.S. gal. tanks, five 1,000-lb. Mk. 83 or 2,000-lb. Mk. 84 bombs, or four AGM-12 Bullpup ASMs.
Status: In production. First of eight test and evaluation aircraft flown April 19, 1960. Deliveries to U.S Navy commenced in 1963.
Notes: A-6A currently serves with both U.S. Navy and U.S. Marine Corps, the latter also operating a countermeasures version, the EA-6A.

GRUMMAN A-6A INTRUDER

Dimensions: Span, 53 ft. 0 in.; length, 54 ft. 7 in.; height, 15 ft. 7 in.; wing area, 529 sq. ft.

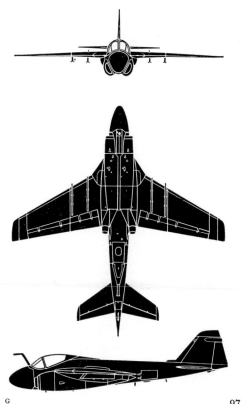

GRUMMAN EA-6B INTRUDER

Country of Origin: U.S.A.
Type: Four-seat All-weather Shipboard Electronic Countermeasures Aircraft.
Power Plants: Two Pratt & Whitney J52-P-8A turbojets each rated at 9,300 lb.s.t.
Performance: (Estimated) Maximum speed, 670 m.p.h. at sea level, 610 m.p.h. at 36,000 ft.; low-level long-range cruising speed (high drag configuration), 345 m.p.h.; low-altitude range (internal fuel), 1,250 mls.
Weights: Empty, 34,581 lb.; maximum loaded, 58,500 lb.
Status: First prototype flown May 25, 1968. Production scheduled to commence 1970, with deployment by U.S. Navy in 1972.
Notes: The EA-6B is a four-seat development of the two-seat EA-6A electronic countermeasures aircraft, retaining the basic aerodynamic design, power plant installation and associated subsystems. The principal change is in the forward fuselage which has been extended by 40 in. in order to allow for the insertion of an additional cockpit accommodating two extra crew members in side-by-side seats, these operating the advanced avionics system, much of which is accommodated in pods beneath the wings and fuselage. These pods contain their own generators which are driven by small airscrews attached to the pods themselves. The EA-6B has sensors which detect, locate, classify and jam enemy radiation.

98

GRUMMAN EA-6B INTRUDER

Dimensions: Span, 53 ft. 0 in.; length, 59 ft. 5 in.; height, 16 ft. 3 in.; wing area, 529 sq. ft.

GRUMMAN G-1159 GULFSTREAM II

Country of Origin: U.S.A.

Type: Corporate Executive Transport.

Power Plants: Two Rolls-Royce RB.163-25 Spey Mk. 511-8 turbofans each rated at 11,400 lb.s.t.

Performance: Maximum cruising speed (at 45,000 lb.), 585 m.p.h. at 40,000 ft.; long-range cruising speed, 496 m.p.h. at 43,000 ft.; maximum climb rate, 5,050 ft./min.; time to 40,000 ft. (at 56,000 lb.), 14·5 min.; range (maximum fuel and reserves for 200-mile diversion plus 30 min. fuel), 3,680 mls., (maximum payload), 1,957 mls. at high-speed cruise, 2,740 mls. at long-range cruise.

Weights: Empty, 32,900 lb.; max. loaded, 57,500 lb.

Accommodation: Normal crew of three and various cabin arrangements for 10–19 passengers.

Status: In production. First prototype flown on October 2, 1966. Initial deliveries late 1967 with production rate of three per month from May 1968. Approximately 85 Gulfstream IIs had been ordered by beginning of 1969 with 40 delivered.

Notes: Optimised for the corporate executive transport role, the Gulfstream II embodies much experience gained with the manufacture of 200 G-159 Gulfstream I turboprop-powered executive transports.

GRUMMAN G-1159 GULFSTREAM II

Dimensions: Span, 68 ft. 10 in.; length 79 ft. 11 in.; height, 42 ft. 6 in.; wing area, 793·5 sq. ft.

HANDLEY PAGE HP.137 JETSTREAM

Country of Origin: United Kingdom.
Type: Light Executive Transport and Feederliner.
Power Plants: Two Turboméca Astazou XIVC turbo-props each rated at 850 e.s.h.p.
Performance: Maximum cruising speed, 298 m.p.h. at 15,000 ft.; long-range cruising speed, 240 m.p.h. at 30,000 ft.; range (maximum fuel, 600-lb. payload and 45 min. reserves), 2,020 mls. at long-range cruising speed, (with 2,330-lb. payload and same reserves), 745 mls. at maximum cruising speed.
Weights: Basic operational, 8,500 lb.; maximum loaded, 12,500 lb.
Accommodation: Flight crew of two and maximum of 18 passengers in high-density feederliner configuration. Alternative interior arrangements for 8–12 passengers.
Status: In production. First of five prototypes flown August 18, 1967. First production example flown December 6, 1968, and production scheduled to attain 15 per month by end of 1969.
Notes: The Jetstream is intended to fulfil corporate executive, feederline and air taxi requirements, and is to be sold primarily through distributors, 65 having been ordered by International Jetstream Corporation and 100 by C.S.E. Aviation. Eleven examples of the Jetstream 3M powered by 895 e.s.h.p. Garrett AiResearch TPE-331-301W turboprops have been ordered by the U.S.A.F. as the C-10A, the first of these being scheduled for delivery spring 1969, the prototype having flown on November 21, 1968.

HANDLEY PAGE HP.137 JETSTREAM

Dimensions: Span, 52 ft. 0 in.; length, 47 ft. 1½ in.;
height, 17 ft. 5½ in.; wing area, 270 sq. ft.

HANDLEY PAGE VICTOR B.(S.R.) MK. 2

Country of Origin: United Kingdom.
Type: Long-range Strategic Reconnaissance and Surveillance Aircraft.
Power Plants: Four Rolls-Royce Conway R.Co.17 Mk. 201 turbofans each rated at 19,750 lb.s.t.
Performance: (Estimated) Maximum speed, 630 m.p.h. at 36,000–50,000 ft. (Mach 0·95); maximum cruising speed, 610 m.p.h. at 55,000 ft.; long-range cruising speed, 560 m.p.h. at 40,000 ft. (Mach 0·85); radius of action (high-altitude mission), 2,300–2,500 mls.; maximum range (with underwing and weapons bay tanks), 5,500–6,000 mls.
Weight: Maximum loaded, 200,000 lb.
Accommodation: Crew of five in pressurised nose compartment. Camera equipment housed in packs mounted in the weapons bay, these packs accommodating a wide variety of camera combinations for day and night reconnaissance and aerial survey. In addition to a camera pack, the weapons bay can house three canisters containing a total of 108 photoflashes, or two photoflash canisters and an auxiliary fuel tank.
Status: Production completed but conversion of B. Mk. 2s to B.(S.R.) Mk. 2s was continuing in 1969.
Notes: The B.(S.R.) Mk. 2 is essentially similar to the B. Mk. 2 (see 1966 edition) phased out in 1968 and can be reconverted for the bombing role.

HANDLEY PAGE VICTOR B.(S.R.) MK. 2

Dimensions: Span, 120 ft. 0 in.; length, 114 ft. 11 in.; height, 30 ft. 1½ in.; wing area, 2,597 sq. ft.

HAWKER SIDDELEY 125 SERIES 400

Country of Origin: United Kingdom.
Type: Light Executive Transport.
Power Plants: Two Rolls-Royce Bristol Viper 522 turbojets each rated at 3,360 lb.s.t.
Performance: Maximum cruising speed, 508 m.p.h. at 31,000 ft.; long-range cruising speed, 449 m.p.h. at 41,000 ft.; range with maximum fuel (1,940-lb. payload and no reserves), 1,992 mls.; maximum climb rate (at 16,000 lb.), 4,800 ft./min.; maximum operating altitude, 41,000 ft.
Weights: Empty equipped, 11,275 lb.; basic operational, 12,260 lb.; maximum loaded, 23,300 lb.
Accommodation: Normal flight crew of two and accommodation for six passengers, but high-density seating arrangements available for maximum of 10 passengers.
Status: In production. The first HS.125-400 (actually the 173rd HS.125 built) was flown in September 1968 and is offered for 1969 delivery.
Notes: The HS.125-400 is a refined version of the Series 3AR (see 1968 edition) incorporating an outward-opening integral airstair door which increases baggage space, an aerodynamically-improved ventral fuselage fairing forward of the wing, and structural changes permitting a 500-lb. increase in maximum take-off weight. Detailed changes include the suppression of most aerials, and some redesign of the flight deck, cabin and vestibule.

HAWKER SIDDELEY 125 SERIES 400

Dimensions: Span, 47 ft. 0 in.; length, 47 ft. 5 in.;
height, 16 ft. 6 in.; wing area, 353 sq. ft.

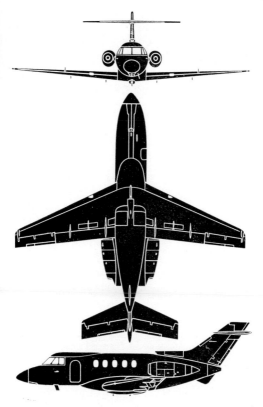

HAWKER SIDDELEY 748 SERIES 2A

Country of Origin: United Kingdom.

Type: Short- and Medium-Range Commercial Transport.

Power Plants: Two Rolls-Royce Dart R.Da.7 Mk. 532-2L turboprops each rated at 2,290 e.s.h.p.

Performance: Maximum speed, 312 m.p.h. at 16,000 ft.; maximum cruising speed, 277 m.p.h. at 15,000 ft.; economical cruising speed, 267 m.p.h. at 20,000 ft.; range cruising speed, 259 m.p.h. at 25,000 ft.; initial climb rate, 1,150 ft./min.; range (with max. fuel and 6,985-lb. payload), 1,957 mls. at 273 m.p.h. at 20,000 ft., (with maximum payload of 11,512 lb. and no reserves), 1,134 mls. at 267 m.p.h. at 20,000 ft.

Weights: Empty, 24,572 lb.; basic operational, 25,988 lb.; maximum loaded, 44,495 lb.

Accommodation: Crew of two plus cabin attendants, and standard cabin arrangement for 40 passengers. High-density arrangement for 58 passengers.

Status: In production. First prototype flown June 24, 1960. First production aircraft (Srs. 1) flown August 30, 1961. Eighteen Srs. 1 aircraft delivered, plus four assembled in India by HAL for Indian Air Force. HAL is also producing 32 Srs. 2 aircraft. Approximately 160 delivered by end of 1968 when production rate was three aircraft per month.

Notes: Series 2A introduced in 1968 with uprated engines and various interior refinements. An HS.748 Series 2 VIP transport of the R.A.A.F. is illustrated above.

108

HAWKER SIDDELEY 748 SERIES 2A

Dimensions: Span, 98 ft. 6 in.; length, 67 ft. 0 in.; height, 24 ft. 10 in.; wing area, 810·75 sq. ft.

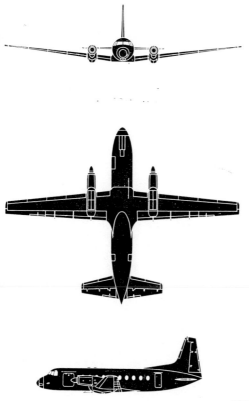

HAWKER SIDDELEY ANDOVER C. MK. 1

Country of Origin: United Kingdom.
Type: Military Tactical Transport.
Power Plants: Two Rolls-Royce Dart R.Da.12 Mk. 210C turboprops each rated at 2,970 s.h.p.
Performance: Maximum speed, 302 m.p.h. at 15,000 ft.; normal cruising speed (at 45,000 lb.), 258 m.p.h. at 20,000 ft.; initial climb rate, 1,170 ft./min.; service ceiling, 24,000 ft.; range (with maximum payload—14,750 lb.), 374 mls., (10,000-lb. payload), 1,186 mls.
Weights: Empty, 26,615 lb.; basic operational, 27,914 lb.; maximum loaded, 50,000 lb.
Accommodation: Flight crew of two or three, and 44 troops, 30 paratroops or 18 casualty stretchers, five sitting casualties and three medical attendants. A 10,500-lb. vehicle may be loaded over the ramp, and 1,200 lb. freight may be carried in flight on the ramp itself.
Status: Production complete. First Andover C. Mk. 1 flown on July 9, 1965, and last of 31 transports of this type completed by end of 1967.
Notes: Evolved from HS.748 (see pages 108–9), the Andover rear-loading transport utilises, with relatively minor modifications, the same forward fuselage and wing. The Andover C. Mk. 1 serves with No. 46 Squadron of R.A.F. Air Support Command's No. 38 Group, and with No. 52 Squadron in the Far East Air Force.

HAWKER SIDDELEY ANDOVER C. MK. 1

Dimensions: Span, 98 ft. 3 in.; length, 77 ft. 11 in.;
height, 30 ft. 1 in.; wing area, 831 sq. ft.

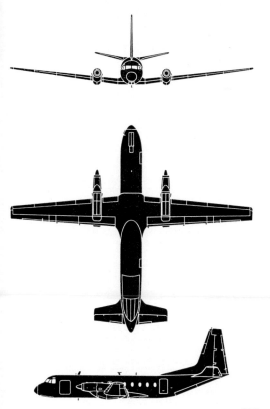

HAWKER SIDDELEY BUCCANEER S.MK.2

Country of Origin: United Kingdom.
Type: Two-seat Shipboard Low-level Strike Aircraft.
Power Plants: Two Rolls-Royce RB.168-1A Spey
R.Sp.2 Mk. 101 turbofans each rated at 11,000 lb.s.t.
Performance: (Estimated) Maximum speed, 700 m.p.h.
at sea level (Mach 0·92); maximum low-level cruising
speed, 665 m.p.h. at 5,000 ft. (Mach 0·9); long-range
cruising speed, 575 m.p.h. at 33,000 ft. (Mach 0·83);
tactical radius (without external fuel), 500–600 mls. for
hi-lo-lo-hi mission; ferry range (with two 250 Imp.
gal./300 U.S. gal. underwing tanks and 750 Imp. gal./
900 U.S. gal. weapons-bay tank), 1,800–2,000 mls.
Weights: Loaded (clean and without weapons), 42,000
lb.; maximum 56,000 lb.
Armament: Four 1,000-lb. bombs or large single store
in weapons bay, and additional offensive stores on four
1,000-lb. capacity underwing pylons. These pylons
may each carry a 1,000-lb. or 500-lb. bomb, 2-in. or
3-in. Glow worm rocket pack, 36-cell MATRA rocket
dispenser, or AGM-12B Bullpup-A ASM.
Status: In production. First of two Spey-powered
pre-production aircraft flown May 17, 1963. First
production S. Mk. 2 flown June 5, 1964. Delivery of
84 to R.N. completed December 1968, and production
of 26 for R.A.F. scheduled to continue until 1971.
Notes: Reconnaissance pack housing six cameras may
be mounted in weapons bay, with Lepus photoflood
flares on wing pylons. With the run-down of its
carrier force, the Royal Navy will transfer approximately 70 Buccaneer S. Mk. 2s to the R.A.F. for
which service further aircraft have been ordered.
These will operate at higher weights, will have a modified undercarriage and various equipment changes.

HAWKER SIDDELEY BUCCANEER S. MK. 2

Dimensions: Span, 44 ft. 0 in.; length, 63 ft. 5 in.;
height, 16 ft. 3 in.; wing area, 514·7 sq. ft.

HAWKER SIDDELEY HARRIER G.R. MK. 1

Country of Origin: United Kingdom.
Type: Single-seat V/STOL Strike and Reconnaissance Fighter.
Power Plant: One Rolls-Royce Bristol Pegasus 101 vectored-thrust turbofan rated at 19,200 lb.s.t.
Performance: (Estimated) Maximum speed, 680–720 m.p.h. (Mach 0·9–0·95) at 1,000 ft., (with typical external ordnance load), 640–660 m.p.h. (Mach 0·85–0·87) at 1,000 ft.; tactical radius (hi-lo-hi mission), 350 mls.; ferry range (with two 212 Imp. gal. ferry tanks), 2,300 mls.; time to 10,000 ft., 40 sec.
Weights: (Estimated) Empty equipped, 12,000 lb.; maximum loaded (VTOL), 16,000 lb., (STOL), 23,000 lb.
Armament: Maximum external load of 5,000 lb. Typical combat load (short-range interdiction) comprises two 30-mm. Aden cannon pods, two 1,000-lb. and two 750-lb. bombs, or two 30-mm. cannon and four MATRA 116 launchers for 68-mm. SNEB missiles.
Status: In production. First of six pre-production aircraft flown August 31, 1966, and first of initial quantity of 60 Harrier G.R. Mk. 1s for R.A.F. flown December 28, 1967. Further 20 Harriers ordered November 1968, this order including both single- and two-seaters.
Notes: Capable of Mach 1·25 in dive. Eleven examples of two-seat Harrier T. Mk. 2 (see opposite page) ordered for training role. Single-seat Harrier Mk. 50 (P.1176 Super Harrier) and two-seat Harrier Mk. 51 to have 21,500 lb.s.t. Pegasus 11 engine.

HAWKER SIDDELEY HARRIER T. MK. 2

Dimensions: (G.R. Mk. 1) Span, 25 ft. 3 in.; length, 46 ft. 4 in.; height, 10 ft. 9 in.; wing area, 201 sq. ft.

HAWKER SIDDELEY NIMROD M.R. MK. 1

Country of Origin: United Kingdom.

Type: Long-range Maritime Patrol Aircraft.

Power Plants: Four Rolls-Royce Spey Mk. 250 turbo-fans each rated at (approx.) 11,500 lb.s.t.

Performance: (Estimated) Maximum cruising speed, 500–530 m.p.h. at 31,000–33,000 ft.; long-range cruising speed, 450–460 m.p.h. at 30,000–35,000 ft.; minimum search speed, 210 m.p.h.; loiter endurance (on two engines), 12–14 hr.

Weights: Maximum loaded, 160,000–170,000 lb.

Armament: Homing torpedoes, depth bombs, etc. in ventral weapons bay, and ASMs on wing pylons.

Accommodation: Normal crew complement of 11 members and (for emergency operation in transport role) 45 troops in rear pressure cabin.

Status: In production. First prototype flown May 23, 1967, and second prototype July 31, 1967. First of 38 production aircraft flown June 28, 1968. First deliveries scheduled for mid-1969.

Notes: The Nimrod employs the basic structure of the Comet 4C transport, the principal change being the addition of an unpressurised pannier to accommodate the weapons bay and permit the retention of the Comet fuselage shell with its known pressurisation characteristics. The pressurised shell has been reduced in length by 6 ft., and the original Avon turbojets have been supplanted by Spey turbofans.

116

HAWKER SIDDELEY NIMROD M.R. MK. 1

Dimensions: Span, 114 ft. 10 in.; length, 126 ft. 9 in.;
height, 29 ft. 8½ in.; wing area, 2,121 sq. ft.

HAWKER SIDDELEY TRIDENT 2E

Country of Origin: United Kingdom.
Type: Medium- to Long-haul Commercial Transport.
Power Plants: Three Rolls-Royce RB.163-25 Spey Mk. 512-5W turbofans each rated at 11,930 lb.s.t.
Performance: Maximum cruising speed, 610 m.p.h. at 25,000 ft., long-range cruising speed, 530 m.p.h. at 35,000 ft., range (with maximum payload—21,378 lb.), 2,430 mls., (with maximum fuel, normal reserves and 16,020-lb. payload), 2,500 mls.
Weights: Basic operational, 72,394 lb.; maximum loaded, 143,500 lb.
Accommodation: Basic flight crew of three and alternative arrangements for 12 first-class and 79 tourist-class passengers, 10 first-class and 88 tourist-class passengers, or 117 tourist-class passengers.
Status: In production. First Trident 2E flown July 27, 1967, and first delivery against order for 15 aircraft of this type to B.E.A. followed February 15, 1968, the first fully-certificated aircraft being handed over on April 17, 1968.
Notes: The Trident 2E differs from the earlier Trident 1C and 1E in having uprated engines, increased weights, flared Kücheman wingtips which cut induced drag and increase overall span by 3 ft., wing and fuselage panels of increased thickness, a strengthened undercarriage, and a 340 Imp. gal. fuel tank in the tail fin. Twenty-six examples of a stretched version, the Trident 3B, are on order for B.E.A. for 1971 service. The Trident 3B has a 131 ft. 2 in.-fuselage for 146 tourist-class or 122 mixed-class passengers, and an RB.162 booster jet in the tail for improved field performance.

118

HAWKER SIDDELEY TRIDENT 2E

Dimensions: Span, 98 ft. 0 in.; length, 114 ft. 9 in.; height, 27 ft. 0 in.; wing area, 1,461 sq. ft.

HAWKER SIDDELEY VULCAN B. MK. 2

Country of Origin: United Kingdom.
Type: Long-Range Medium Bomber.
Power Plants: Four Bristol Siddeley Olympus B.Ol.21
Mk. 301 turbojets each rated at 20,000 lb.s.t.
Performance: (Estimated) Maximum speed, 645 m.p.h.
at 40,000–45,000 ft. (Mach 0·98); maximum cruising
speed, 620 m.p.h. at 45,000 ft. (Mach 0·94); maximum
cruising altitude, 55,000 ft.; tactical radius (for
hi-lo-lo-hi sortie profile), 1,700 mls., (at 40,000–55,000
ft.), 2,300 mls.; maximum range, 4,750 mls.
Weights: Loaded, 180,000–200,000 lb.
Armament: Twenty-one 1,000-lb. general-purpose
bombs, or free-fall nuclear weapons.
Status: Production completed. First B. Mk. 2 flown
August 19, 1958, deliveries to R.A.F. Bomber Command (now incorporated in Strike Command) commencing July 1960. Production completed 1964.
Notes: Equipping the eight bomber squadrons of No.
1 Group R.A.F. Strike Command, the Vulcan B. Mk.
2 was originally conceived for the high-altitude role
but its mission capability has now been extended to
include low-level penetration, and it is expected to
remain in first-line service until the mid-'seventies,
although from 1969 its primary role is tactical, and the
Blue Steel stand-off missile formerly carried by some
aircraft has been phased out of service. To be placed
at the disposal of N.A.T.O. for long-range tactical
strike missions with conventional weapons, the Vulcan
squadrons have a declining responsibility as the
R.A.F.'s main strike element. The Vulcan B. Mk. 2
was preceded by 45 examples of the B. Mk. 1.

HAWKER SIDDELEY VULCAN B. MK. 2

Dimensions: Span, 111 ft. 0 in.; length, 99 ft. 11 in.; height, 27 ft. 2 in.; wing area, 3,964 sq. ft.

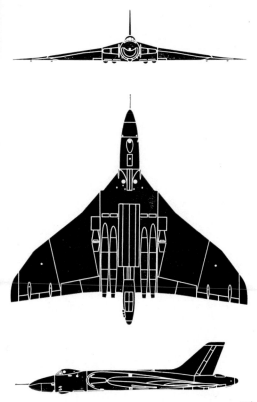

HISPANO HA-200E SUPER SAETA 41

Country of Origin: Spain.
Type: Advanced Trainer and Light Tactical Strike and Reconnaissance Aircraft.
Power Plants: Two Turboméca Marboré VI turbojets each rated at 1,058 lb.s.t.
Performance: Maximum speed, 413 m.p.h. at sea level, 429 m.p.h. at 22,965 ft.; maximum cruising speed, 341 m.p.h. at sea level, 360 m.p.h. at 19,685 ft.; economical cruising speed, 336 m.p.h. at sea level, 348 m.p.h. at 19,685 ft.; range (with maximum fuel and no reserves), 466 mls. at sea level, 932 mls. at 29,530 ft.; initial climb rate, 3,050 ft./min.; service ceiling 42,650 ft.
Weights: Empty equipped, 4,453 lb.; maximum loaded, 7,937 lb.
Armament: Two 7·7-mm. machine guns in forward fuselage, and two MATRA 38 universal attachments for various stores, including camera or rocket pods, rocket launchers, or bombs.
Status: Prototype (converted from first production HA-200D) flown early 1965, and series production envisaged for 1970.
Notes: The Super Saeta is a more powerful derivative of the HA-200D Saeta (see 1966 edition), with more extensive avionics, beefed-up undercarriage, and re-designed air intakes. It is being preceded in production by a single-seat light strike variant, the HA-220, the manufacture of 25 examples began in 1968 with the completion of the last of 55 HA-200Ds.

HISPANO HA-200E SUPER SAETA 41

Dimensions: Span, 34 ft. 2 in., (over tip tanks), 35 ft. 10 in.; length, 29 ft. 5 in.; height, 9 ft. 4 in.; wing area, 187·2 sq. ft.

I.A.I. ARAVA

Country of Origin: Israel.
Type: Light Utility Transport and Feederliner.
Power Plants: Two Pratt & Whitney PT6A-27 turbo-props each rated at 620 s.h.p.
Performance (Estimated) Maximum speed, 217 m.p.h. at 10,000 ft.; maximum cruising speed, 211 m.p.h. at 10,000 ft.; economical cruising speed, 186 m.p.h.; range (maximum fuel and 30 min. reserves), 810 mls., (maximum payload—4,410 lb.), 311 mls.; initial climb rate, 1,720 ft./min.; service ceiling, 27,900 ft.
Weights: Operational empty, 7,055 lb.; maximum loaded, 12,500 lb.
Accommodation: Flight crew of one or two, and maximum of 20 passengers in four-abreast rows, or 12 casualty stretchers and two medical attendants in the ambulance role.
Status: First of eight pre-production examples scheduled to commence flight test programme April 1969, and the first production model is expected to be delivered in March 1970, a production rate of four per month being attained in 1971.
Notes: The Arava features a full-width rear cargo door hinged to swing sideways at truck-bed height, and is intended to fulfil a variety of roles, both civil and military, and an order is expected to be placed on behalf of the Israel Defence Forces.

124

I.A.I. ARAVA

Dimensions: Span, 68 ft. 7 in.; length, 42 ft. 7¼ in.;
height, 17 ft. 0¾ in.; wing area, 470·2 sq. ft.

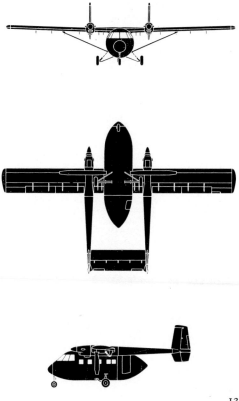

IAR-821

Country of Origin: Rumania.
Type: Light Agricultural and Utility Monoplane.
Power Plant: One Ivchenko AI-14MRF nine-cylinder radial air-cooled engine rated at 300 h.p.
Performance: (Figures in parentheses relate to aircraft equipped for spraying) Maximum speed, 133 (121) m.p.h. at sea level; maximum cruising speed, 127 (112) m.p.h. at 4,920 ft.; economical cruising speed, 110 (99) m.p.h.; range at economical cruise with 1,323-lb. payload, 342 mls.; service ceiling, 21,325 (13,125) ft.
Weights: Empty, 2,337 lb.; maximum loaded, 4,189 lb.
Accommodation: Pilot in enclosed cockpit with steel-tube turn-over structure and jettisonable upward-hinging glazed side panels. Standard agricultural equipment includes a 176 Imp. gal. or 1,323-lb. capacity hopper immediately ahead of the cockpit.
Status: Prototype flown early 1968. Initial production deliveries scheduled to commence mid-1969.
Notes: The IAR-821 has been designed by Radu Manicatide, chief of the aircraft design bureau of URMV-3, the aviation section of the general engineering Sovromtractor concern, formerly the Industria Aeronautica Romana (IAR). Radu Manicatide has been responsible for the design of the IAR-817 and 818 utility monoplanes manufactured in small quantities and several versions. A tandem two-seat version of the IAR-821, the IAR-821B, completed state trials in 1968, and is scheduled to enter series production during 1969.

IAR-821

Dimensions: Span, 41 ft. 11½ in.; length, 30 ft. 2 in.; height, 9 ft. 1½ in.; wing area, 279·86 sq. ft.

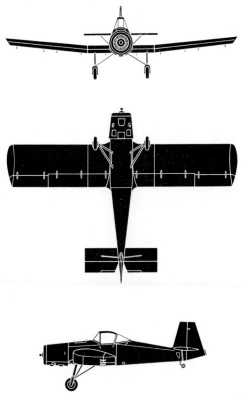

ILYUSHIN IL-62 (CLASSIC)

Country of Origin: U.S.S.R.
Type: Long-range Commercial Transport.
Power Plants: Four Kuznetsov NK-8-4 turbofans
each rated at 23,150 lb.s.t.
Performance: Maximum cruising speed, 540 m.p.h. at
32,810 ft.; long-range cruising speed, 520 m.p.h. at
32,810 ft.; range with maximum fuel and 22,046-lb.
payload plus one hour's reserves, 5,717 mls., with maximum payload—50,706 lb., 4,163 mls.; initial climb
rate (at 340,610 lb.), 3,937 ft./min., (at 352,740 lb.),
3,543 ft./min.; time to 32,810 ft. (at 352,740 lb.), 21
min.; normal operational altitude, 36,090 ft.
Weights: Empty operational, 148,812 lb.; maximum
loaded, 352,740 lb.
Accommodation: Flight crew of five and arrangements
for 186 passengers in high-density layout, 168 passengers in tourist-class layout, and 115 passengers in
first-class layout.
Status: In production. First of two prototypes flown
January 1963, production being initiated late in 1965.
Notes: The Il-62 entered service with Aeroflot in 1967,
the inaugural Moscow–Montreal Il-62 service being
operated on September 15, 1967. The Kuznetsov
NK-8-3 turbofans of the initial production version
have been supplanted by the improved NK-8-4 which
in turn, are expected to give place to 25,353 lb.s.t
Soloviev D-30K turbofans during 1970–71. A 204
passenger stretched version, the Il-62M, is scheduled
for Aeroflot service from 1971. This will have additional fuselage sections increasing overall length by
21 ft. 4 in.

ILYUSHIN IL-62 (CLASSIC)

Dimensions: Span, 142 ft. 0¾ in.; length, 174 ft. 2½ in.; height, 40 ft. 8 in.; wing area, 3,037·57 sq. ft.

IPD-6504 BANDEIRANTE

Country of Origin: Brazil.

Type: Light Utility Transport.

Power Plants: Two Pratt & Whitney PT6A-20 turbo-props each rated at 550 s.h.p.

Performance: (Estimated) Maximum speed, 282 m.p.h. at 10,000 ft.; maximum cruising speed, 267 m.p.h. at 8,200 ft.; maximum range (with 30 min. reserves), 1,120 mls. at 16,400 ft.; initial climb rate, 1,770 ft./min.; service ceiling, 29,500 ft.

Weights: Empty equipped, 5,620 lb.; maximum loaded, 9,920 lb.

Accommodation: (Prototype) Flight crew of two and seven–nine passengers. It is anticipated that the production version will incorporate a lengthened fuselage to provide accommodation for a maximum of 14 passengers.

Status: First of four prototypes was flown for the first time on October 22, 1968. Series production against order for 24 to commence 1970.

Notes: The Bandeirante has been designed by a team led by Max Holste (designer of the Nord 262) at the Departmento de Aeronaves (PAR) of the Instituto de Pesquisas e Desenvolvimento (IPD) which, in turn, is a division of the governmental Centro Técnico de Aeronáutica. It is intended to meet a Brazilian Air Force requirement, and it is anticipated that some 80 will be ordered for utility, ambulance, and navigational training roles. A derivative, the Maraba seating up to 30 passengers, is proposed as a C-47 replacement.

IPD-6504 BANDEIRANTE

Dimensions: Span, 50 ft. 7 in.; length, 41 ft. 9½ in.; height, 16 ft. 11½ in.; wing area, 314 sq. ft.

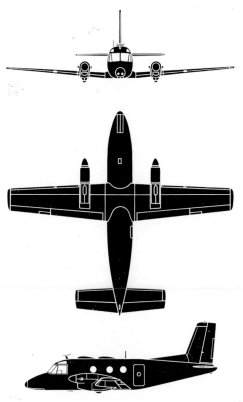

IS-23

Country of Origin: Rumania.
Type: Light STOL Utility Aircraft.
Power Plant: One Ivchenko AI-14RF nine-cylinder radial air-cooled engine rated at 300 h.p.
Performance: Maximum speed, 127 m.p.h. at sea level; maximum cruising speed, 112 m.p.h. at 4,920 ft.; economical cruising speed, 96 m.p.h.; initial climb rate (at maximum loaded weight), 787 ft./min., (at 4,190 lb.), 964 ft./min.; service ceiling (at 4,519 lb.), 15,750 ft., (at 4,012 lb.), 18,045 ft.
Weights: Empty, 2,976 lb.; maximum loaded, 4,630 lb.
Accommodation: Cabin may be arranged to accommodate five passengers or two casualty stretchers and a medical attendant.
Status: Prototype trials initiated mid-1968.
Notes: The IS-23 has been designed by Professor Iosif Silmov, previously known as a designer of medium- and high-performance sailplanes, to meet an official specification for a light utility aircraft suitable for ambulance, agricultural, glider-towing, and other tasks, and possessing short-take-off-and-landing characteristics. Of all-metal construction, the IS-23 carries all fuel (22 Imp. gal.) in wing tanks, and extensive use is made of high lift devices to achieve a take-off distance of 131–202 yards and a landing distance of 65–87 yards, landing speed being 43–50 m.p.h. Floats or skis may replace the wheel undercarriage.

IS-23

Dimensions: Span, 40 ft. 8¼ in.; length, 29 ft. 10¼ in.; height, 11 ft. 9¾ in.

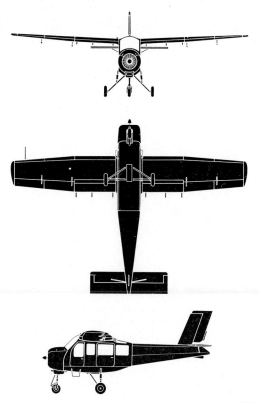

L 29A DELFIN AKROBAT

Country of Origin: Czechoslovakia.
Type: Single-seat Aerobatic Trainer.
Power Plant: One M 701 turbojet rated at 1,918 lb.s.t.
Performance: Maximum speed, 394 m.p.h. at sea level,
415 m.p.h. at 16,400 ft.; long-range cruising speed,
290 m.p.h. at 16,400 ft.; maximum range (internal fuel),
440 mls.; initial climb rate, 3,405 ft./min.; time to
16,400 ft., 7 min.; service ceiling, 43,960 ft.
Weights: Normal loaded, 5,732 lb.
Status: Prototype L 29A Delfin Akrobat flown initially
early 1968. It is anticipated that the single-seat L 29A
will be phased into the existing two-seat L 29 production line during 1969. Approximately 2,200 Delfins
of all versions had been manufactured by the beginning
of 1969, production rate being 16–17 aircraft monthly,
peak production having reached 42 per month in 1967.
Delfin production is currently scheduled to continue
into 1971.
Notes: The Delfin Akrobat is a single-seat version of
the Delfin two-seat basic trainer (see 1966 edition),
the rear cockpit and most avionics being removed, and
a slightly derated version of the M 701 engine installed. Variants of the standard Delfin include the
L 29R light tactical reconnaissance and counter-
insurgency aircraft which, in addition to serving with
the Czechoslovak Air Force, has been supplied to
Uganda and Nigeria. Code-named *Maya* by N.A.T.O.,
the Delfin is the standard Soviet Air Force basic
trainer, and has also been supplied to the air arms of
Bulgaria, Hungary, Indonesia, Rumania, East Germany, the U.A.R., Syria and Iraq.

L 29A DELFIN AKROBAT

Dimensions: Span, 33 ft. 9 in.; length, 35 ft. 5½ in.; height, 10 ft. 3 in.; wing area, 213·1 sq. ft.

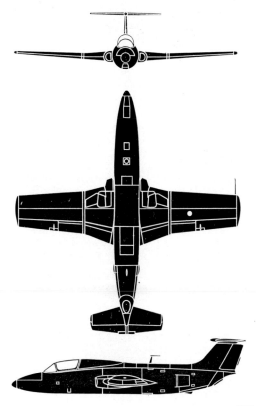

L39

Country of Origin: Czechoslovakia.
Type: Tandem Two-seat Basic Trainer.
Power Plant: One Walter Titan (Ivchenko AI-25V)
turbofan rated at 3,307 lb.s.t.
Performance: No details of the performance of the L 39
had been revealed at the time of closing for press, but
it is known that the Soviet specification to which the
L 39 was designed called for a high subsonic performance.
Weights: No details available.
Status: Three prototypes constructed, the first being a
static test specimen and the second flying for the first
time on November 4, 1968. The third prototype was
scheduled to join the flight test programme late 1968
or early 1969.
Notes: The L 39 has been designed to meet the requirements of a Soviet specification calling for a
successor to the L 29 Delfin (see pages 134–135) as a
standard " Warsaw Pact " basic trainer, and will
eventually be evaluated in competition with a Soviet-
designed trainer evolved to meet the requirements of
the same specification. The L 39 has secondary
attack capabilities, and both single- and two-seat
variants for the light reconnaissance-attack role are
envisaged. If 1970 competitive evaluation is success-
ful, the L 39 will supplant the L 29 Delfin in the
Warsaw Pact air forces training syllabus from 1972–73.

L 39

Dimensions: Span, 29 ft. 9⅞ in.; length 39 ft. 7½ in.; height, 14 ft. 5¼ in.

L 410 TURBOLET

Country of Origin: Czechoslovakia.
Type: Light Utility Transport and Feederliner.
Power Plants: Two M 601 turboprops each rated at 700 s.h.p.
Performance: (Estimated) Maximum speed, 239 m.p.h. at 9,840 ft.; maximum cruising speed, 224 m.p.h. at 9,840 ft.; range with 30 min. reserves and 3,968-lb. payload, 373 mls., with 2,645-lb. payload, 620 mls.; initial climb rate, 1,675 ft./min.
Weights: Empty equipped, 6,400 lb.; maximum loaded, 11,250 lb.
Accommodation: Flight crew of two, and 12–17 passengers in three-abreast seating.
Status: Prototype scheduled to fly late June 1969, with production deliveries commencing in 1971.
Notes: First prototype powered by 652 e.s.h.p. Pratt & Whitney PT6A-27 turboprops pending uprating of M 601 currently rated at 550 e.h.p. Tentative order on behalf of the Czechoslovak Air Force for 40 for liaison and training tasks. Stretched version proposed with lengthened fuselage capable of accommodating 22–25 passengers.

L 410 TURBOLET

Dimensions: Span, 56 ft. 1¼ in.; length, 44 ft. 3½ in.; height, 18 ft. 0½ in.; wing area, 349·827 sq. ft.

LFU 205

Country of Origin: Federal Germany.
Type: Light Cabin Monoplane.
Power Plant: One Lycoming IO-360-A1C four-cylinder horizontally-opposed engine rated at 200 h.p.
Performance: Maximum speed, 223 m.p.h. at sea level; maximum cruising speed, 186 m.p.h.; range (at 75% power), 880 mls. at 177 m.p.h.; initial climb rate, 1,082 ft./min.; service ceiling, 19,500 ft.
Weights: Empty, 1,543 lb.; loaded, 2,645 lb.
Accommodation: Four persons in two side-by-side pairs of seats beneath aft-sliding canopy.
Status: First prototype flown March 29, 1968. Currently experimental programme to prove constructional techniques.
Notes: Developed by the Leichtflugtechnik-Union (LFU) formed by the Bölkow, Putzer and Rhein-Flugzeugbau concerns, the LFU 205 is built entirely of glass-fibre reinforced plastic. Representing the end product of a number of years of research into the use of highly-stressed reinforced plastics for the primary components of powered aircraft, the LFU 205 uses a semi-sandwich skin consisting of a smooth outer skin bonded to a corrugated inner skin. The corrugations run chordwise in the wings and tail surfaces, thus forming a large number of ribs, and framewise in the fuselage, resulting in a pure monocoque structure.

LFU 205

Dimensions: Span, 35 ft. 7¼ in.; length, 25 ft. 1¼ in.; height, 8 ft. 0¾ in.; wing area, 176 sq. ft.

LING-TEMCO-VOUGHT A-7D CORSAIR II

Country of Origin: U.S.A.

Type: Single-seat Tactical Strike Fighter.

Power Plant: One Allison TF41-A-1 (Rolls-Royce RB.168-62 Spey) turbofan rated at 14,250 lb.s.t.

Performance: Maximum speed (no external stores and 60% fuel), 699 m.p.h. (Mach 0·92) at sea level, (with 12 250-lb. Mk. 81SE bombs), 633 m.p.h., (with 10 750-lb. M 117 bombs), 604 m.p.h.; tactical radius (internal fuel and one hour on station for hi-lo-hi mission with 12 Mk. 81SE bombs), 512 mls. at average cruising speed of 532 m.p.h., (with 10 M 117 bombs), 390 mls. at average cruising speed of 509 m.p.h.; ferry range (internal fuel), 2,775 mls., (with four 250 Imp. gal. drop tanks), 3,880 mls.; initial climb rate (no external stores and 60% fuel), 13,550 ft./min.

Weights: Empty equipped, 17,747 lb.; maximum loaded (without external ordnance), 30,000 lb.; maximum overload, 43,720 lb.

Armament: One 20-mm. M-61A-1 rotary cannon with 1,000 rounds, plus maximum external ordnance load (for short-range interdiction) of 15,000 lb. on eight stations.

Status: In production. First A-7D (with TF30-P-6) flown April 6, 1968. First A-7D (with TF41-A-1) flown September 26, 1968. Deliveries to U.S.A.F. scheduled to commence 1969, with first Tactical Air Command wing attaining operational status in 1970.

Notes: The A-7D is a land-based derivative of the U.S. Navy's A-7 (see 1968 edition) with new engine, increased armour, revised avionics, etc. The U.S. Navy's A-7E will have a 15,000 lb.s.t. TF41-A-2 turbofan and similar avionics to the A-7D.

LING-TEMCO-VOUGHT A-7D CORSAIR II

Dimensions: Span, 38 ft. 8¾ in.; length, 46 ft. 1½ in.; height, 16 ft. 2 in.; wing area, 375 sq. ft.

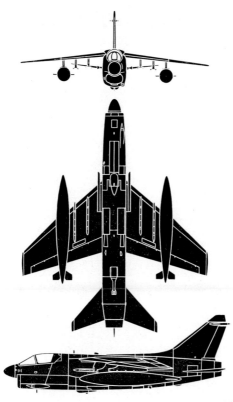

LOCKHEED C-5A GALAXY

Country of Origin: U.S.A.

Type: Long-range Military Strategic Transport.

Power Plants: Four General Electric TF39-GE-1 turbofans each rated at 41,000 lb.s.t.

Performance: (Estimated) Maximum cruising speed, 540 m.p.h.; long-range cruising speed, 506 m.p.h.; range at long-range cruise, (with 265,000-lb. payload), 3,110 mls., (with 220,000-lb. payload), 3,510 mls., (with 100,000-lb. payload), 6,680 mls.; initial climb rate (at 712,000 lb.), 2,150 ft./min.

Weights: Operational empty, 323,904 lb.; normal loaded, 728,000 lb.; maximum, 764,500 lb.

Accommodation: Basic flight crew of six plus relief crew of six, courier seating for eight plus 75 troops in compartment above cargo hold. Typical loads include two 4·46-ton trucks and ammunition trailers; two Iroquois helicopters; one M41 or M551 tank; two Minuteman missiles in shipping and storage containers mounted on transporters. Maximum payload is 265,000 lb.

Status: In production. First of eight test and evaluation aircraft flown June 30, 1968. Current order for 58 C-5As with Nos. 9–24 scheduled for delivery by end of 1969. Options taken on further 142 for U.S.A.F. to follow on initial 58 to be completed by end of 1970.

Notes: Current plans call for U.S.A.F. Military Airlift Command to operate six squadrons of 16 Galaxies, with first squadron to be formed at Charleston A.F.B. October–December 1969. Small number of C-5As expected to be ordered for the R.A.F.

144

LOCKHEED C-5A GALAXY

Dimensions: Span, 222 ft. 7¼ in.; length, 245 ft. 10¾ in.; height, 65 ft. 1¼ in.; wing area, 6,200 sq. ft.

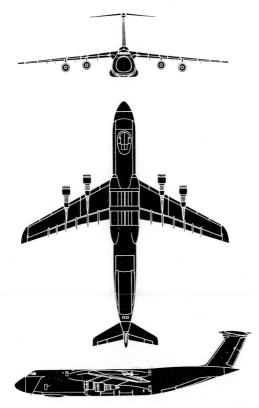

LOCKHEED (C-130K) HERCULES C. MK. 1

Country of Origin: U.S.A.

Type: Military Strategic Transport.

Power Plants: Four Allison T56-A-15 turboprops each rated at 4,910 e.s.h.p.

Performance: Maximum cruising speed, 385 m.p.h.; normal cruising speed, 340 m.p.h.; initial climb rate (at 155,000 lb.), 1,880 ft./min.; range (maximum payload—45,901 lb.), 2,430 mls., (maximum fuel and 20,259-lb. payload), 4,780 mls.

Weights: Maximum loaded, 155,000 lb.

Accommodation: Normal crew of five plus 92 troops, 62 paratroops, or 74 casualty stretchers plus two medical attendants.

Status: In production. First C-130K flew October 19, 1966, contracts calling for 66 aircraft of this type completed 1968. Approximately 1,040 C-130s of all types delivered by the beginning of 1969, the 1,000th (an HC-130H for the U.S. Coast Guard) being delivered on April 26, 1968.

Notes: C-130K is version for R.A.F. for which some sub-assemblies have been manufactured by Scottish Aviation in the U.K. As the Hercules C. Mk. 1, it serves with Nos. 24, 30, 36 and 47 Squadrons of R.A.F. Air Support Command's No. 38 Group. The C-130K is essentially similar to the C-130H for the R.N.Z.A.F., and, apart from the power plants, to the C-130E which is the principal U.S.A.F. version.

146

LOCKHEED (C-130K) HERCULES C. MK. 1

Dimensions: Span, 132 ft. 7¼ in.; length, 99 ft. 6 in.;
height, 38 ft. 2½ in.; wing area, 1,745 ft.

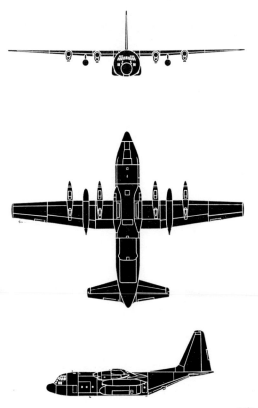

LOCKHEED C-141A STARLIFTER

Country of Origin: U.S.A.

Type: Military Strategic Transport.

Power Plants: Four Pratt & Whitney TF33-P-7 turbofans each rated at 21,000 lb.s.t.

Performance: Maximum speed, 570 m.p.h.; maximum cruising speed, 562 m.p.h.; long-range cruising speed, 506 m.p.h.; initial climb rate, 3,200 ft./min.; service ceiling (at 250,000 lb.), 40,000 ft.; range (with 70,847-lb. payload), 3,973 mls., (with maximum fuel and 30,877-lb. payload), 6,045 mls.; ferry, 6,822 mls.

Weights: Empty equipped, 133,773 lb.; max. loaded, 316,100 lb.

Accommodation: Normal flight crew of four, and a maximum of 154 troops, 123 paratroops, or 80 casualty stretchers and eight medical attendants. Up to 5,283 cu. ft. of freight may be loaded on 10 pallets.

Status: In production. First test and evaluation aircraft flown December 17, 1963, and first delivery to U.S.A.F. Military Airlift Command on October 20, 1964, the 289th and last being delivered on February 28, 1968.

Notes: The StarLifter equips 14 Military Airlift Command squadrons, the last of which, the 30th Military Airlift Squadron, began re-equipping in August 1967.

148

LOCKHEED C-141A STARLIFTER

Dimensions: Span, 160 ft. 1 in.; length, 145 ft. 0 in.;
height, 39 ft. 4 in.; wing area, 3,228 sq. ft.

LOCKHEED F-104S STARFIGHTER

Country of Origin: U.S.A.

Type: Single-seat Interceptor and Strike Fighter.

Power Plant: One General Electric J79-GE-19 turbojet rated at 11,870 lb.s.t. and 17,900 lb.s.t. with afterburning.

Performance: Maximum speed, 1,450 m.p.h. at 40,000 ft. (Mach 2·2), 915 m.p.h. at 1,000 ft. (Mach 1·2); cruising speed, 610 m.p.h. at 36,000 ft. (Mach 0·92); initial climb rate, 50,000+ ft./min.; combat ceiling, 57,000 ft.; tactical radius (with two 162 Imp. gal./200 U.S. gal. and two 100 Imp. gal./120 U.S. gal. drop tanks), 740–775 mls.; ferry range, 2,200 mls.

Weights: Empty, 14,573 lb.; loaded (clean), 21,307 lb.; max. loaded, 31,000 lb.

Armament: One 20-mm. M-61 Vulcan rotary cannon and two AIM-7 Sparrow III semi-active radar homing and two AIM-9 Sidewinder infra-red homing AAMs.

Status: In production. First of two F-104S prototypes flown December 1966. Production of 165 in Italy with orders placed for 82 by beginning of 1969, the first having been rolled out on October 30, 1968.

Notes: The F-104S is a derivative of the F-104G (see 1966 edition) intended primarily for the all-weather intercept role. Two prototypes have been modified by the parent company from Italian-manufactured F-104G airframes, and licence manufacture is being undertaken for the Italian Air Force by Fiat.

LOCKHEED F-104S STARFIGHTER

Dimensions: Span, 21 ft. 11 in.; length, 54 ft. 9 in.;
height, 13 ft. 6 in.; wing area, 196·1 sq. ft.

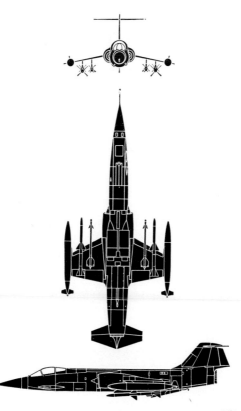

LOCKHEED P-3B ORION

Country of Origin: U.S.A.

Type: Long-range Maritime Patrol Aircraft.

Power Plants: Four Allison T56-A-14 turboprops each rated at 4,910 e.s.h.p. (4,591 s.h.p.).

Performance: (At 105,000 lb.) Maximum speed, 476 m.p.h. at 15,000 ft.; normal cruising speed, 397 m.p.h. at 25,000 ft.; initial climb rate, 3,270 ft./min.; loiter endurance (four engines) at 1,500 ft., 12·9 hr., (two engines), 17 hr.; maximum mission radius (3 hr. on station at 1,500 ft.), 2,533 mls.

Weights: Empty, 60,000 lb.; max. loaded, 127,200 lb.

Accommodation: Normal crew of 12 comprising pilot, co-pilot, flight engineer, radio operator, navigator, sonobuoy operator, radar/MAD operator, Julie/ECM operator, tactical co-ordinator, ordnanceman, and two relief members, and for emergency troop carrier role up to 50 combat troops and 4,000 lb. of equipment.

Armament: Weapons bay can accommodate two Mk. 101 nuclear depth bombs and four Mk. 43, 44 or 46 torpedoes, or eight Mk. 54 bombs. All 10 external pylons can carry torpedoes, mines or rockets, maximum external stores load being 13,713 lb.

Status: In production. YP-3A prototype flown on November 25, 1959, and first pre-production P-3A flown April 15, 1961.

Notes: P-3B ordered by R.N.Z.A.F. (5) and R.A.A.F. (10). The P-3C features advanced avionics, maximum and overload weights of 133,500 lb. and 142,000 lb. and 24 will be delivered during 1969.

152

LOCKHEED P-3B ORION

Dimensions: Span 99 ft. 8 in.; length, 116 ft. 10 in.; height, 33 ft. 8½ in.; wing area, 1,300 sq. ft.

McDONNELL F-4E PHANTOM II

Country of Origin: U.S.A.

Type: Two-seat Tactical Strike Fighter.

Power Plants: Two General Electric J79-GE-17 turbojets each rated at 11,870 lb.s.t. and 17,900 lb.s.t. with afterburning.

Performance: Maximum speed (without external stores), 1,580 m.p.h. at 40,000 ft. (Mach 2·4), 910 m.p.h. at sea level (Mach 1·2); initial climb rate, 30,000 ft./min.; low-level tactical radius (eight 750-lb. bombs and two 308 Imp. gal. drop tanks), 400 mls. at 420 m.p.h.; ferry range, 2,300 mls. at 575 m.p.h. at 40,000 ft.

Weights: Empty, 30,425 lb.; normal loaded, 46,297 lb.; max. loaded, 60,630 lb.

Armament: One 20-mm. General Electric M-61A1 rotary cannon and up to 16,000 lb. of external stores, typical loads including 15 1,000-lb. Mk. 83, 18 750-lb. M-117, or 24 500-lb. Mk. 82 bombs, four AGM-12 Bullpup ASMs, or 15 LAU-3A or 13 LAU-10A rocket launchers.

Status: In production. First F-4E flown on June 30, 1967, and first to U.S.A.F. on October 3, 1967.

Notes: The F-4E is the production successor to the F-4D (see 1967 edition) from which it differs in having an extended nose housing an improved and miniaturised APQ-120 fire control radar system and recessed pod with a multiple-barrel M-61A1 cannon, uprated engines and additional fuel. Fifty F-4Es are to be delivered to Israel, licence production is to be undertaken in Japan, and 88 examples of a reconnaissance version, the RF-4E, are on order for Germany.

McDONNELL F-4E PHANTOM II

Dimensions: Span, 38 ft. 4¾ in.; length, 62 ft. 10 in.; height, 16 ft. 3 in.; wing area, 530 sq. ft.

McDONNELL PHANTOM F.G.R. MK 2.

Country of Origin: U.S.A.

Type: Two-seat Strike and Reconnaissance Fighter.

Power Plants: Two Rolls-Royce RB.168-25R Spey R.Sp. 5R Mk. 201 turbofans each rated at 12,500 lb.s.t. and 20,100 lb.s.t. with afterburning.

Performance: Maximum speed (with four AIM-7E Sparrow III AAMs), 1,386 m.p.h. at 40,000 ft. (Mach 2·1), 910 m.p.h. at sea level (Mach 1·2); service ceiling, 60,000 ft.; low-level tactical radius (with six 1,000-lb. bombs or equivalent external load), 500 mls.; ferry range, 2,500 mls.

Weights: Approx. empty, 30,000 lb; maximum loaded, 56,000 lb.

Armament: (Strike) Combinations of missiles, such as the AS.37 and AJ.168 Martel, AGM-12 Bullpup, etc., and bombs. (Intercept) Four or six AIM-7E Sparrow III semi-active radar-homing AAMs.

Status: In production. The first of two (YF-4M) prototypes flown on February 17, 1967, and deliveries against orders for 116 commenced August 1968.

Notes: Anglicised shore-based R.A.F. equivalent of U.S. Navy's F-4J and similar to F-4K or Phantom F.G.R. Mk. 1 (see 1967 edition) for Royal Navy.

156

McDONNELL PHANTOM F.G.R. MK. 2

Dimensions: Span, 38 ft. 4 in.; length, 57 ft. 11 in.; height, 16 ft. 3⅓ in.; wing area, 530 sq. ft.

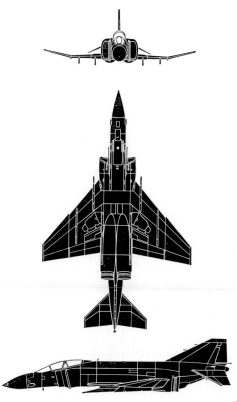

MHK-101

Country of Origin: Federal Germany.
Type: Light Cabin Monoplane.
Power Plant: One Lycoming O-235-C2A four-cylinder horizontally-opposed engine rated at 115 h.p.
Performance: Maximum speed, 149 m.p.h. at sea level; cruising speed (75% power), 137 m.p.h.; range, 497 mls.; initial climb rate, 827 ft./min.; service ceiling, 14,765 ft.
Weights: Empty, 970 lb.; loaded (aerobatic) 1,150 lb., (utility), 1,810 lb.
Accommodation: Side-by-side seating for two persons on single bench.
Status: Prototype flown December 22, 1967. Production expected to commence (as Bö 209) in 1969.
Notes: The MHK-101 has been designed by a group of Bölkow engineers in their spare time, the designation 'MHK' resulting from the first letters of the surnames of the leaders of the project, Hans Mylius, Walter Heynen, and Hans Kraus. The MHK-101 has folding wings and has been designed for towing along roads, an unusual feature being the fixed main undercarriage members and *retractable* nosewheel, the latter intended primarily to simplify towing. With an increased wing span (28 ft. 2½ in.) it is proposed to manufacture the MHK-101 in series as the Bölkow 209, a projected development, the MHK-102 which may be produced as the Bölkow 210, having inward-retracting mainwheels, a stub wing extending overall span to 31 ft. 2½ in. and housing additional fuel, and Lycoming O-320 or IO-320 engines being offered as alternatives.

MHK-101

Dimensions: Span, 26 ft. 8¾ in.; length 20 ft. 0⅞ in.; height, 7 ft. 5¾ in.; wing area, 104·4 sq. ft.

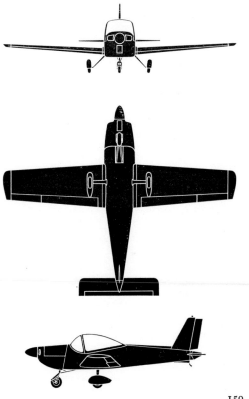

MIKOYAN MIG-21PF (FISHBED-F)

Country of Origin: U.S.S.R.

Type: Single-seat All-weather Interceptor Fighter.

Power Plant: One TDR R.37F turbojet rated at approximately 10,000 lb.s.t. and 13,200 lb.s.t. with afterburning.

Performance: Maximum speed (without external stores), 1,450 m.p.h. at 36,000–40,000 ft. (Mach 2·2), (with two Atoll AAMs or UV-16-57 rocket pods), 1,320 m.p.h. (Mach 2·0); subsonic cruise tactical radius (without external fuel), 400 mls.; time to 40,000 ft., 4·5 min.

Weights: (Estimated) loaded (with one 132 Imp. gal. centreline drop tank and two Atoll missiles), 17,700 lb.; maximum loaded, 19,500 lb.

Armament: Two Atoll AAMs or two UV-16-57 pods each housing 16 55-mm. rockets.

Status: In production. Licence manufacture undertaken in Czechoslovakia and India (latter producing MiG-21FL).

Notes: In its latest form, the MiG-21PF embodies a number of modifications (illustrated by the drawing on the opposite page), including vertical tail surfaces of increased chord, a repositioned braking chute housing, and a new cockpit canopy with separate quarter lights and hood. The export version of the MiG-21PF, the MiG-21FL, differs from the standard model only in avionic equipment, and the MiG-21F (Fishbed-C) is the standard day interceptor model. A tandem two-seat training version of the fighter, the MiG-21UTI (Mongol), was described and illustrated in the 1968 edition.

MIKOYAN MIG-21PF (FISHBED-F)

Estimated Dimensions: Span, 25 ft. 0 in.; length, 49 ft. 0 in.; height, 15 ft. 0 in.; wing area, 250 sq. ft.

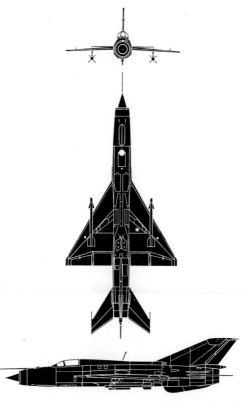

MIKOYAN MIG-23 (FOXBAT)

Country of Origin: U.S.S.R.
Type: Single-seat Interceptor and Strike Fighter.
Power Plants: Two turbojets each rated at approx.
22,000 lb.s.t. and 33,000 lb.s.t. with afterburning.
Performance: (Estimated) Maximum speed (short-period dash), 2,110 m.p.h. at 40,000-50,000 ft. (Mach 3·2), 910 m.p.h. at sea level (Mach 1·2).
Weights: Approximate loaded, 90,000 lb.
Status: In production. Believed flown in prototype form 1963–64 with first service deliveries 1967.
Notes: The Foxbat, designated MiG-23 in service form, has established a number of internationally-recognised records as the Ye-266, the first of these being announced in April 1965 and being a 1,000-km. closed circuit record of 1,441·5 m.p.h. (Mach 2·2) carrying a 4,409-lb. payload, the flight being performed between 69,000 and 72,200 ft. In October 1967, the Ye-266 attained 98,458 ft. with a 4,409-lb. payload and covered a 500-km. closed circuit at an average speed of 1,820·6 m.p.h. (Mach 2·76), and on November 4, 1967 averaged 1,807 m.p.h. over a 1,000-km. circuit. The MiG-23 is expected to attain service status in the strike role during the course of 1969, and in the high-altitude intercept role during 1970–71.

MIKOYAN MIG-23 (FOXBAT)

Estimated Dimensions: Span, 47 ft. 0 in.; length, 85 ft.
0 in.; height, 20 ft. 0 in.; wing area, 830 sq. ft.

MIKOYAN FAITHLESS

Country of Origin: U.S.S.R.
Type: Single-seat STOL Fighter-Bomber.
Power Plants: One turbojet of 25,000–30,000 lb.s.t.
with afterburning and two vertically-disposed lift
engines.
Performance: Presumed to be capable of speeds of the
order of Mach 2·2–2·5.
Weights: Believed to be in the 40,000–45,000 lb.
loaded weight category.
Status: Believed experimental. Prototypes probably
tested during 1966–67, but this type is not believed
to have attained production status.
Notes: The short take-off and landing single-seat
fighter bomber made its public début at Domodedovo
on July 9, 1967, when a single prototype was demonstrated. In addition to the single large cruise engine,
two vertical lift engines are mounted in the fuselage aft
of the cockpit to reduce take-off and landing runs, but
there is some evidence to suggest that development
was initiated as a conventional type, the lift engines
being added as a second phase. The *Faithless* may have
been evolved to meet the same requirement which has
apparently been met by the Sukhoi-designed *Flagon*
(see pages 234–5).
164

MIKOYAN FAITHLESS

Estimated Dimensions: Span, 30 ft. 0 in.; length (including nose probe), 62 ft. 0 in.; height, 15 ft. 0 in.

MIKOYAN FLOGGER

Country of Origin: U.S.S.R.

Type: Single-seat Tactical Strike and Reconnaissance Fighter.

Power Plant: One turbojet rated at 28,000–30,000 lb.s.t. with afterburning.

Performance: (Estimated) Maximum speed, 1,650 m.p.h. at 40,000 ft. (Mach 2·5), 910 m.p.h. at sea level (Mach 1·2).

Weights: Approximate loaded, 40,000–45,000 lb.

Status: Believed experimental. Single prototype demonstrated at Domodedovo July 1967. Current status uncertain. Possible service introduction 1969–1970.

Notes: Appreciably smaller and lighter than the General Dynamics F-111 and approximating more closely to the Dassault Mirage G, the Mikoyan-designed variable-geometry fighter was believed to have attained a relatively early development stage at the time of closing for press. The wing design follows U.S. first generation practice closely in that the hinge points are set well out from the fuselage and large fixed wing-root gloves are provided. The wing reportedly translates from the full-forward low-speed position to the full-aft high-speed position in some four seconds. The rectangular air intakes are noteworthy, and the vertical tail surfaces are augmented at high speeds by a large ventral fin which appears to fold sideways for take-off and landing.

166

MIKOYAN FLOGGER

Estimated Dimensions: Span (minimum sweep), 48 ft.
0 in., (maximum sweep), 24 ft. 0 in.; length (including
probe), 60 ft. 0 in.; height, 15 ft. 0 in.

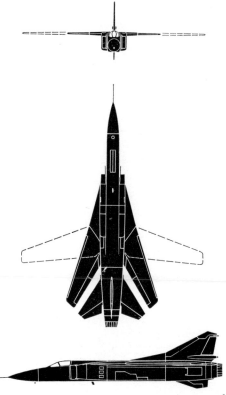

MITSUBISHI MU-2F

Country of Origin: Japan.

Type: Light Executive and Utility Transport.

Power Plants: Two Garrett AiResearch TPE-331-151A turboprops each rated at 665 s.h.p.

Performance: Maximum cruising speed, 340 m.p.h. at 10,000 ft.; economical cruising speed, 291 m.p.h. at 20,000 ft.; maximum range (with 30 min. reserves and full payload), 1,550 mls. at 23,000 ft.; initial climb rate, 2,875 ft./min.; service ceiling, 30,400 ft.

Weights: Empty equipped, 5,780 lb.; maximum loaded, 9,920 lb.

Accommodation: Standard version provides pressurised cabin for pilot and six passengers, but an alternative arrangement is available for eight passengers.

Status: In production. Deliveries of MU-2F commenced mid-1968. and it was anticipated that more than 80 MU-2s of all versions would be delivered by the beginning of 1969.

Notes: MU-2F differs from its production predecessor, the MU-2D, in having larger wingtip tanks and more powerful engines, the earlier model having differed from the initial production MU-2B in having integral wing tanks. A stretched version of the MU-2F featuring a 5 ft. 1¼ in. increase in fuselage length, permitting up to 11 passengers to be accommodated in high-density seating, is designated MU-2G, and two prototypes were scheduled to commence flight trials early in 1969.

MITSUBISHI MU-2F

Dimensions: Span, 39 ft. 2 in.; length, 33 ft. 3 in. height, 12 ft. 11 in.; wing area, 178 sq. ft.

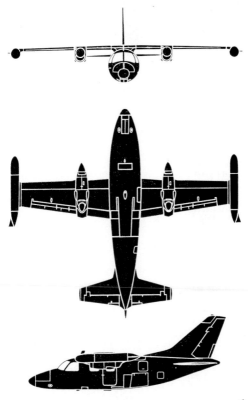

NAMC YS-11A

Country of Origin: Japan.
Type: Short- and Medium-range Commercial Transport.
Power Plants: Two Rolls-Royce Dart 542-10 turbo-props rated at 2,660 e.h.p. (dry) and 3,060 e.h.p. (wet).
Performance: Maximum cruising speed, 291 m.p.h. at 15,000 ft.; economical cruising speed, 281 m.p.h. at 20,000 ft.; range (maximum fuel and no reserves), 1,310 mls., (maximum payload—15,320 lb.), 680 mls.; initial climb rate, 1,220 ft./min.; service ceiling, 22,900 ft.
Weights: Operational empty (YS-11A-200), 33,180 lb., (YS-11A-300), 33,840 lb.; maximum loaded, 54,010 lb.
Accommodation: Basic flight crew of two and (YS-11A-200) standard seating for 60 passengers, or (YS-11A-300) 46 passengers and 540 cu. ft. cargo space.
Status: In production. First YS-11A flown November 27, 1967. Production rate of 3·5 per month by beginning of 1969 and 70 YS-11As scheduled for completion by August 1968.
Notes: The YS-11A series has been developed from the original YS-11-100, 50 examples of which were produced, the 51st and subsequent machines being to YS-11A standards. The principal variants are the YS-11A-200 (illustrated above), the mixed passenger freight YS-11A-300 (illustrated on the opposite page), and the all-freight YS-11A-400. One example of the last-mentioned version has been acquired by the Maritime Self-Defence Force, flying for the first time on February 17, 1968. The YS-11T is an ASW trainer variant of the YS-11A-200.

NAMC YS-11A

Dimensions: Span, 104 ft. 11¾ in.; length, 86 ft. 3½ in. height, 29 ft. 5¾ in.; wing area, 1,020·4 sq. ft.

NEIVA IPD-6201 UNIVERSAL

Country of Origin: Brazil.

Type: Basic Training Monoplane.

Power Plant: One Lycoming IO-540-G1A5 six-cylinder horizontally-opposed engine rated at 290 h.p.

Performance: (Specification relates to aircraft at utility weight, figures in parentheses relating to aircraft at aerobatic weight) Maximum speed, 193 (195) m.p.h. at sea level; maximum cruising speed, 180 (184) m.p.h. at 6,560 ft.; range at 75% power with 10% reserves, 1,180 (620) mls. at 13,000 ft.; initial climb rate, 1,575 (1,730) ft./min.; service ceiling, 21,650 (26,250) ft.

Weights: Empty equipped, 2,314 lb.; loaded (utility), 3,640 lb., (aerobatic), 3,085 lb.

Accommodation: Two seats side by side with full dual controls beneath aft-sliding canopy. Optional third seat at rear.

Status: First of two prototypes flown April 29, 1966. Series production scheduled to commence 1969, with initial deliveries to Brazilian Air Force in 1970.

Notes: The Universal was designed by Josef Kovacs to meet a Brazilian Air Force requirement for a replacement for the T-6 Texan basic trainer, and the service has a total requirement for 150 Universal trainers which are expected to begin to supplant the T-6 at the Escola de Aeronáutica at Pirassununga from 1970. Preparations for series production were being made by the Sociedade Construtora Aeronáutica Neiva at the end of 1968.

172

NEIVA IPD-6201 UNIVERSAL

Dimensions: Span, 36 ft. 1 in.; length, 27 ft. 10½ in.;
height, 10 ft. 2 in.; wing area, 183 sq. ft.

NORD 262

Country of Origin: France.

Type: Light Commercial Transport.

Power Plants: Two Turboméca Bastan VIC turbo-props each rated at 1,065 e.s.h.p.

Performance: Maximum speed, 239 m.p.h. at 14,990 ft.; economical cruising speed (70% power), 224 m.p.h. at 16,400 ft.; initial climb rate, 1,160 ft./min.; service ceiling, 24,000 ft.; range (maximum fuel and 4,426-lb. payload), 690 mls., (with maximum payload —6,400 lb.), 200 mls.

Weights: Empty operational, 15,123 lb.; maximum loaded, 22,707 lb.

Accommodation: Crew of two and seating for 26 passengers in standard version. Alternative arrangements available for 29 passengers. Movable bulkhead caters for variable cargo-passenger configuration.

Status: In production. Prototype flown December 24, 1962, and first production model flown May 7, 1963. First production aircraft to definitive standards flown on June 10, 1964. Production of 70 authorised, and production rate was two per month by mid-1968, approximately 48 having been delivered by the beginning of 1969.

Notes: Intended as a DC-3 replacement, the pressurised Nord 262 is also suitable for military roles, and France's *Aéronavale* has ordered two and taken an option on a further 13 for light transport and crew training tasks, and six have been delivered to the *Armée de l'Air.*

NORD 262

Dimensions: Span, 71 ft. 10¼ in.; length, 63 ft. 3 in.; height, 20 ft. 4 in.; wing area, 592 sq. ft.

NORD 500

Country of Origin: France.
Type: Single-seat Tilt-duct VTOL Research Aircraft.
Power Plants: Two Allison T63-A-5A shaft turbines each rated at 317 s.h.p.
Performance: (Estimated) Maximum speed, 217 m.p.h. at sea level; cruising speed, 175 m.p.h.
Weights: Maximum loaded, 2,760 lb.
Status: Prototype development. First prototype began static tests in April 1967, and second prototype effected the first vertical take-off (tethered) on July 23, 1968.
Notes: The Nord 500 tilting-duct research aircraft is of generally similar concept to the Bell X-22A (see 1966 edition). The short-span fixed surfaces are carried by a raised boom which also houses the side-by-side T63-A-5A shaft turbines driving the five-bladed ducted airscrews via interconnected shafts. For vertical take-off and landing the ducts are tilted to horizontal position. Conventional cockpit controls are provided, control in yaw and pitch being achieved by differential and collective duct tilting respectively, and thrust modulation being employed for roll control. With completion of hovering and transition trials, Stage 2 development during 1969 will include controlled and variable expansion of the duct flow.

Dimensions: Span, 20 ft. 1½ in.; length, 21 ft. 7 in.; height, 10 ft. 1½ in.

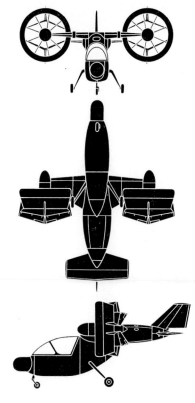

NORTH AMERICAN ROCKWELL
OV-10A BRONCO

Country of Origin: U.S.A.

Type: Tandem Two-seat Light Counter-insurgency and Forward Air Control Aircraft.

Power Plants: Two Garrett-AiResearch T76-G-10/12 turboprops each rated at 715 s.h.p.

Performance: Maximum speed, 279 m.p.h. at sea level, 259 m.p.h. at 20,000 ft.; average cruising speed, 194 m.p.h.; tactical radius (close support strike mission at 12,500 lb., including 1 hr. loiter in target area, with 146 Imp. gal.), 110 mls., (with 210 Imp gal.), 215 mls., (with 335 Imp. gal.), 390 mls.; ferry range, 1,310 mls.; initial climb rate, 2,320 ft./min.

Weights: Empty, 7,076 lb.; normal loaded, 11,340 lb.; maximum, 12,500 lb.

Armament: Four 7·62-mm. M-60C machine guns with 500 r.p.g., plus various combinations of ordnance on one 1,200-lb. and four 600-lb. capacity external stations. U.S. Marine Corps model also has wing pylons for two AIM-9D Sidewinder missiles.

Status: In production. First of seven prototypes flown July 16, 1965, and first production aircraft flown August 6, 1967. Deliveries to both U.S.A.F. and U.S.M.C. initiated February 23, 1968 against orders for 109 and 114 for the respective services.

Notes: Bronco began operational service in Vietnam with both U.S.A.F. and U.S.M.C. in July 1968. Eighteen to be delivered to German Army as target-tugs, most having an auxiliary J85 turbojet to boost maximum speed to 375 m.p.h. for high-speed target towing.

178

NORTH AMERICAN ROCKWELL
OV-10A BRONCO

Dimensions: Span, 40 ft. 0 in.; length (including pitot head), 41 ft. 7 in.; height, 15 ft. 1 in.; wing area, 291 sq. ft.

179

NORTH AMERICAN ROCKWELL
COURSER COMMANDER

Country of Origin: U.S.A.

Type: Light Business Executive Transport.

Power Plants: Two Lycoming IGSO-540-B1C six-cylinder horizontally-opposed engines each rated at 380 h.p.

Performance: Maximum speed 240 m.p.h.; cruising speed (75% power), 225 m.p.h. at 16,000 ft., (65% power), 215 m.p.h. at 10,000 ft.; maximum range (with optional auxiliary tankage of 50 Imp. gal.), 1,300 mls. at 55% power at 10,000 ft., (with standard tankage), 1,160 mls., initial climb rate, 1,282 ft./min.; service ceiling, 27,500 ft.

Weights: Empty, 5,449 lb., maximum loaded, 8,500 lb.

Accommodation: Flight crew of one or two and standard accommodation for six passengers in cabin. Alternative arrangement (Courser Liner) for nine passengers.

Status: In production. Courser Commander introduced May 1968 as a stretched, higher-powered equivalent of the Shrike Commander introduced simultaneously, the latter being previously known as the Aero Commander 500U.

Notes: The Courser Commander is a refined development of the unpressurised version of the former Grand Commander embodying some features of the former Turbo II Commander (e.g. lengthened nose and panoramic windows).

180

NORTH AMERICAN ROCKWELL
COURSER COMMANDER

Dimensions: Span, 49 ft. 2½ in.; length, 42 ft. 3¼ in.; height, 14 ft. 6 in.; wing area, 255 sq. ft.

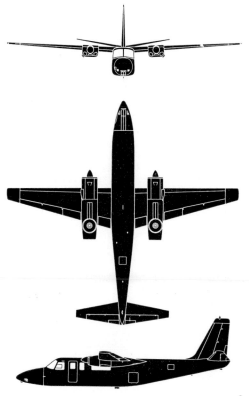

NORTH AMERICAN ROCKWELL
LARK COMMANDER

Country of Origin: U.S.A.

Type: Light Cabin Monoplane.

Power Plant: One Lycoming O-360-A2F four-cylinder horizontally-opposed engine rated at 180 h.p.

Performance: Maximum speed, 138 m.p.h. at sea level; cruising speed (75% power), 132 m.p.h. at 7,500 ft.; maximum range, 525 mls.; initial climb rate, 750 ft./min.; service ceiling, 13,000 ft.

Weights: Empty, 1,450 lb., maximum loaded, 2,450 lb.

Accommodation: Four seats in two pairs, and 120-lb. capacity baggage compartment.

Status: In production. Introduced in May 1968 as refined, more powerful version of Aero Commander 100 which, in turn, was a redesign of the Volair 1050.

Notes: The Lark Commander, or Model 100/180, is structurally similar to the Model 100/150, originally known as the Aero Commander 100 and now named Darter Commander. Apart from a more powerful engine (the Darter Commander having a 150 h.p. Lycoming O-320-A), the Lark Commander differs in having swept vertical tail surfaces, detail refinements to reduce drag, and a de luxe cabin interior finish. The basic design was originally developed by the Volaircraft Corporation.

NORTH AMERICAN ROCKWELL
LARK COMMANDER

Dimensions: Span, 35 ft. 0 in.; length, 24 ft. 11 in.;
height, 10 ft. 1 in.; wing area, 180 sq. ft.

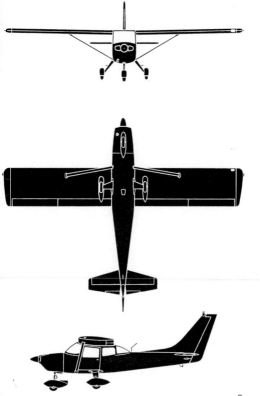

NORTH AMERICAN ROCKWELL SNIPE COMMANDER

Country of Origin: U.S.A.

Type: Agricultural Monoplane.

Power Plant: One Pratt & Whitney IR-985 Wasp nine-cylinder radial air-cooled engine rated at 450 h.p.

Performance: Maximum speed, 119 m.p.h. at sea level; cruising speed (at 3,000 lb. and 75% power), 115 m.p.h.; operating speed, 90–100 m.p.h.; initial climb rate (at 4,500 lb.), 650 ft./min.

Weights: Empty, 2,700 lb.; loaded, 4,500 lb.; maximum (CAR Part 8*), 5,400 lb. *Permissible in excess of certificated gross weight.

Accommodation: Single seat aft of 250 Imp. gal./2,400 lb.-capacity hopper, and provision for carrying mechanic or loader on ferry flights.

Status: In production. Derivative of Ag Commander B-1 introduced April 1968.

Notes: The Snipe Commander is a re-engined version of the Ag Commander B-1 (400 h.p. Lycoming IO-720-A1A horizontally-opposed engine) which had originally flown on January 15, 1966, as the IMCO CallAir B-1, and was taken over by North American Rockwell, together with the CallAir A-9, a smaller agricultural aircraft (290 h.p. Lycoming IO-540-G1C5) now known as the Quail Commander, and, with a lower-powered engine (235 h.p. Lycoming O-540-B2B5), as the Sparrow Commander.

184

NORTH AMERICAN ROCKWELL
SNIPE COMMANDER

Dimensions: Span, 44 ft. 0 in.; length, 30 ft. 0 in.; height, 10 ft. 0 in.; wing area, 280 sq. ft.

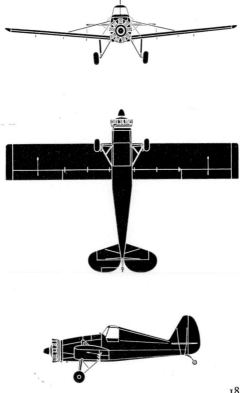

NORTH AMERICAN ROCKWELL RA-5C VIGILANTE

Country of Origin: U.S.A.

Type: Tandem Two-seat Shipboard Strategic Reconnaissance and Attack Bomber.

Power Plants: Two General Electric J79-GE-10 turbojets each rated at 11,870 lb.s.t. and 17,900 lb. with afterburning.

Performance: Maximum speed, 1,385 m.p.h. at 40,000 ft. (Mach 2·1); maximum stabilised speed (without external stores), 1,254 m.p.h. (Mach 1·9); maximum low-level cruising speed, 633 m.p.h. (Mach 0·83); long-range cruising speed, 560 m.p.h. at 40,000 ft. (Mach 0·85); operational ceiling, 64,000 ft.; maximum range, 2,995 mls.

Weights: Loaded, 61,730 lb.; max. overload, 74,000 lb.

Armament: The RA-5C normally fulfils the reconnaissance role but possesses secondary attack capability, each of four external pylons being capable of lifting a 2,500-lb. load of offensive stores.

Status: Production, originally terminated in 1963, reinstated in 1967 and scheduled to continue through 1971. Prototype RA-5C flown June 30, 1962. Remaining A-5A Vigilantes subsequently brought up to RA-5C standards.

Notes: The RA-5C carries an extremely sophisticated reconnaissance system, including vertical, oblique, and split-image cameras, and SLAR (Side-Looking Airborne Radar) in removable modules. Aircraft delivered from April 1969 will have uprated J79-GE-10 engines and enlarged wing root leading edge fillets.

NORTH AMERICAN ROCKWELL
RA-5C VIGILANTE

Dimensions: Span, 53 ft. 0 in.; Length, 75 ft. 10 in.; height, 19 ft. 4¾ in.; wing area, 700 sq. ft.

PILATUS PC-8 TWIN PORTER

Country of Origin: Switzerland.

Type: Light STOL Utility Transport.

Power Plants: Two Lycoming IO-540-G1B5 six-cylinder horizontally-opposed engines each rated at 290 h.p.

Performance: (Estimated) Maximum speed, 162 m.p.h. at 8,000 ft.; maximum cruising speed (70%) power, 143 m.p.h. at 8,000 ft.; economical cruising speed (65% power), 140 m.p.h.; maximum range (with 1,590-lb. payload), 680 mls.; initial climb rate, 1,200 ft./min.

Weights: Empty, 3,420 lb.; maximum loaded, 5,950 lb.

Accommodation: Pilot and nine passengers.

Status: First of two prototypes flown November 28, 1967. Production deliveries expected to commence in 1970.

Notes: Development of the Twin-Porter has been delayed pending a definitive choice of engines, and at the time of closing for press, various changes intended for the production model were being incorporated in a second prototype. Much of the airframe of the Twin-Porter is based on that of the single-engined PC-6 Porter, and similar short-take-off-and-landing characteristics are offered. Large double-doors are incorporated in each side of the fuselage to facilitate the loading of freight.

PILATUS PC-8 TWIN-PORTER

Dimensions: Span, 51 ft. 2½ in.; length, 34 ft. 7¼ in.;
height, 12 ft. 0 in.; wing area, 348 sq. ft.

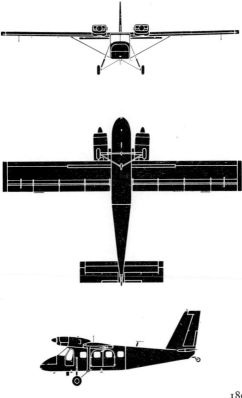

PIPER PA-35 POCONO

Country of Origin: U.S.A.

Type: Light Executive Transport and Feederliner.

Power Plants: Two Lycoming TIo-720-A1A eight-cylinder horizontally-opposed engines each rated at 470 h.p.

Performance: (Estimated) Maximum speed, 242 m.p.h. at 10,000 ft.; maximum cruising speed (75% power), 216 m.p.h. at 10,000 ft.; 230 m.p.h. at 17,000 ft.; range with 45 min. reserves (at 75% power), 650 mls., (55% power), 810 mls.; initial climb rate, 1,630 ft./min.

Weights: Empty equipped (freighter), 4,650 lb., (18-seat feederliner), 4,900 lb.; maximum loaded, 9,000 lb.

Accommodation: Basic arrangements for pilot and 13 or 17 passengers as feederliner, or crew of two and up to 11 passengers as executive transport. As a freighter the useful load is 4,350 lb.

Status: Prototype flown for first time on May 13, 1968, and first production deliveries scheduled for early 1970.

Notes: The largest aircraft yet built by Piper, the Pocono is intended primarily for the third-level scheduled-service and light freighter market. The specification applies to the prototype (which is illustrated), but the production Pocono will have 520 h.p. engines and a gross weight of 9,750 lb. Modifications necessary to meet performance specifications have delayed commencement of production.

PIPER PA-35 POCONO

Dimensions: Span, 51 ft. 0 in.; length, 39 ft. 3 in.; height, 15 ft. 9 in.; wing area, 315 sq. ft.

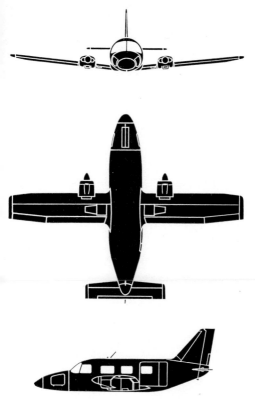

PZL-104 WILGA 32

Country of Origin: Poland.

Type: Light Utility Aircraft.

Power Plant: One Continental O-470-L six-cylinder horizontally-opposed engine rated at 230 h.p.

Performance: Maximum speed, 127 m.p.h. at sea level; economical cruising speed, 93 m.p.h.; range, 342 mls. at 93 m.p.h., 435 mls. at 84 m.p.h.; initial climb rate, 885 ft./min.; service ceiling, 15,500 ft.

Weights: Empty, 1,631 lb.; maximum loaded, 2,712 lb.

Accommodation: Four persons in pairs, or pilot, medical attendant and two casualty stretchers.

Status: In production. Wilga 32 (O-470-L) and Wilga 35 (AI-14R) introduced in 1968 as refined developments of the Wilga C and Wilga 3. Original Wilga 1 prototype flown April 24, 1962, followed by the extensively redesigned Wilga 2 on August 1, 1963, production deliveries commencing as the Wilga C and Wilga 3 in 1966. Wilga C assembled in Indonesia from imported components as the Gelatik, with order for 56 examples scheduled for completion in 1969.

Notes: The Wilga 32 (illustrated and described) and Wilga 35 are essentially similar apart from the power plant, the latter having a 260 h.p. Ivchenko AI-14R nine-cylinder air-cooled radial, and versions of both models are available for agricultural, ambulance, glider-towing, light freighter, and other roles.

PZL-104 WILGA 32

Dimensions: Span, 36 ft. 4¾ in.; length, 26 ft. 9¼ in.; height, 8 ft. 2½ in.; wing area, 166·8 sq. ft.

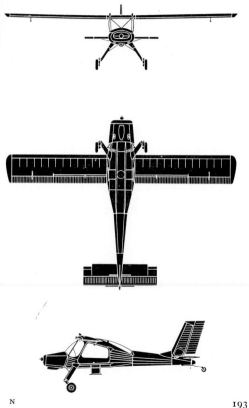

RYAN XV-5B

Country of Origin: U.S.A.
Type: Experimental Single-seat Research Aircraft.
Power Plants: Two General Electric J85-GE-5 turbo-jets each rated at 2,658 lb.s.t. driving (for take-off and landing) two wing-mounted General Electric X353-5B lift fans and one nose-mounted X376 lift fan which, with exit louvres vectored aft, boost total static thrust to 8,400 lb. and provide 7,200 lb. lift.
Performance: Maximum speed (jet mode), 525 m.p.h., (fan mode), 103 m.p.h.; maximum cruising speed (jet mode), 460 m.p.h. at 40,000 ft.; economical cruising speed (jet mode), 345 m.p.h.; maximum sideward speed (fan mode), 33 m.p.h.
Weights: Empty equipped, 9,150 lb.; maximum loaded, 12,326 lb.
Status: Sole example of XV-5B (originally second XV-5A) affected first conventional flight on July 15, 1968.
Notes: The XV-5B is engaged in a National Aeronautics and Space Administration-sponsored lift fan research and development programme at the Ames Research Centre. A reconstruction and modification of the second of two XV-5As which was damaged during an emergency landing in October 1966, the XV-5B differs from the -5A primarily in having the main undercarriage members moved outboard of the wing fans (the undercarriage initially being non-retractable), improved ejector seat, cockpit arrangement and fuel system, and the thrust spoiler mechanism removed.

RYAN XV-5B

Dimensions: Span, 29 ft. 10 in.; length, 44 ft. 6¼ in.;
height, 14 ft. 9 in.; wing area, 260·32 sq. ft.

SAAB 35X DRAKEN

Country of Origin: Sweden.

Type: Single-seat Tactical Fighter-Bomber.

Power Plant: One Svenska Flygmotor RM 6C (Rolls-Royce RB.146 Mk. 60 Avon) rated at 12,710 lb.s.t. and 17,260 lb.s.t. with afterburning.

Performance: Maximum speed (without external stores), 1,320 m.p.h. at 36,000–40,000 ft. (Mach 2·0); initial climb rate (clean), 39,510 ft./min.; tactical radius (with nine 1,000-lb. bombs, 14 500-lb. bombs or four rocket pods) at high altitude at Mach. 0·9 including five min. combat at low altitude, 230 mls., at low altitude at 495 m.p.h., 150 mls., (with two 280 and two 110 Imp. gal. drop tanks plus two 1,000-lb. or four 500-lb. bombs), 700 mls. at high altitude and 400 mls. at low altitude; ferry range (with four 280 Imp. gal. drop tanks), 2,015 mls.

Weights: Maximum loaded, 35,270 lb.

Armament: Two 30-mm. Aden M/55 cannon and maximum external ordnance load of 9,000 lb.

Status: In production for Denmark. Current production versions for Swedish Air Force are the J 35F interceptor and S 35E tactical reconnaissance aircraft.

Notes: The Saab 35X is an export version of the basic Draken which will enter Danish service in 1970, 20 strike fighter, 20 reconnaissance-fighter, and six two-seat trainer models having been ordered. Flown for the first time in the summer of 1967, the Saab 35X is optimised for the lo-lo-lo attack mission over extended ranges, and differs from the J 35F (see 1967 edition) in having additional internal tankage. Existing weapons hard points have been repositioned and provision made for additional hard points.

196

SAAB 35X DRAKEN

Dimensions: Span, 30 ft. 10¾ in.; length (excluding
nose probe), 46 ft. 10¼ in.; height, 12 ft. 8⅓ in.; wing
area, 529·8 sq. ft.

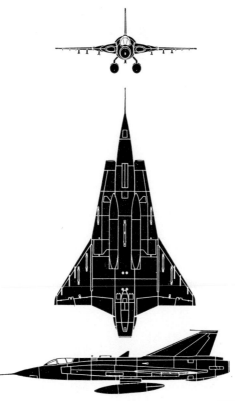

SAAB 37 VIGGEN

Country of Origin: Sweden.

Type: Single-seat (JA 37) Interceptor and (AJ 37) Strike Fighter, (S 37) Tactical Reconnaissance Aircraft, and (Sk 37) Two-seat Advanced Trainer.

Power Plant: One Svenska Flygmotor RM 8 (Pratt & Whitney JT8D-22) turbofan rated at approx. 16,000 lb.s.t. and 26,450 lb.s.t. with afterburning.

Performance: (Approximate) Maximum speed, 835 m.p.h. at 330 ft. (Mach 1·1), 1,320 m.p.h. at 39,370 ft. (Mach 2·0); time to 36,090 ft. at 33,060 lb., 2 min.; service ceiling, 60,000 ft.

Weight: Normal loaded, 35,275 lb.

Armament: (Attack mission) Rb 04C or RB 05A attack missiles or pods containing six 13·5-cm. or 19 7·5-cm. rockets, or 30-mm. Aden cannon, or 1,000-lb bombs on five external pylons. (Intercept mission) Rb 24, Rb 27 or Rb 28 AAMs.

Status: First of seven prototypes flown February 8, 1967, and four under test by end of 1968. Seventh prototype will be two-seat trainer. Production orders placed by beginning of 1969 for 175 aircraft. First delivery scheduled for July 1, 1971, with completion of initial order for 100 aircraft (83 AJ 37s and 17 Sk 37s) by beginning of 1974.

Notes: Versions of Viggen to be covered by follow-on contracts uncertain at time of closing for press but include the S 37, the future of the JA 37 interceptor with secondary attack capability being under review.

198

SAAB 37 VIGGEN

Dimensions: Span, 34 ft. 9¼ in., length (including nose probe), 53 ft. 5¾ in., height, 18 ft. 4½ in.

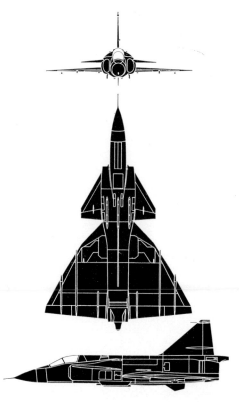

SAAB 105XT

Country of Origin: Sweden.
Type: Basic Trainer and Light Strike and Reconnaissance aircraft.
Power Plants: Two General Electric J85-GE-17B turbojets each rated at 2,850 lb.s.t.
Performance: Maximum speed (at 8,818 lb.) 604 m.p.h. at sea level, 547 m.p.h. at 32,810 ft.; tactical radius with six 500-lb. bombs (lo-lo-lo mission), 200 mls., (hi-lo-hi), 514 mls., with four 500-lb. bombs and two 108 Imp. gal. drop tanks (lo-lo-lo), 325 mls., (hi-lo-hi), 845 mls., range (at 437 m.p.h. at 36,000 ft. with 20 min. reserves), 1,380 mls., (with two 108 Imp. gal. drop tanks), 1,715 mls.; initial climb rate (at 8,818 lb.), 12,795 ft./min., (at 10,802 lb.), 9,055 ft./min.; service ceiling (at 8,818 lb.), 44,950 ft.
Weights: Empty, 5,550 lb.; normal loaded (clean), 9,750 lb.; maximum loaded, 14,328 lb.
Armament: Maximum of 4,410 lb. of ordnance on six underwing pylons. Typical loads include two 30-mm. cannon pods and two sidewinder AAMs, four 500-lb. and two 1,000-lb. bombs, or 12 13·5-cm. rockets.
Status: In production. Prototype Saab 105XT flown April 29, 1967. First deliveries (against order for 20) to Austria scheduled Spring 1970.
Notes: The Saab 105XT is an export version of the basic Saab 105 which (with two 1,640 lb.s.t. Turboméca Aubisque turbofans) serves with the Swedish Air Force as the SK 60A trainer, SK 60B trainer with attack capability, and SK 60C trainer with attack and photo-reconnaissance capability.

SAAB 105XT

Dimensions: Span, 31 ft. 2 in.; length, 34 ft. 5$\frac{1}{3}$ in.; height, 8 ft. 10$\frac{1}{4}$ in.; wing area, 175·515 sq. ft.

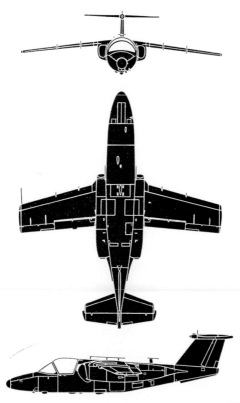

SEPECAT JAGUAR

Countries of Origin: United Kingdom and France.

Type: (Jaguar A and S) Single-seat Tactical Strike Fighter and (Jaguar B and E) Two-seat Advanced Trainer.

Power Plants: Two Rolls Royce Turboméca RB.172/T.260 Adour turbofans each rated at (approx.) 4,400 lb.s.t. and 6,600 lb.s.t. with afterburning.

Performance: Maximum speed, 820 m.p.h. (Mach 1·1) at 1,000 ft., 1,120 m.p.h. (Mach 1·7) at 40,000 ft.; low-level cruise, 530–680 m.p.h. (Mach 0·7–0·9); tactical radius (lo-lo-lo mission on internal fuel with typical load, e.g., two 1,000-lb. bombs and four MATRA 18-rocket pods), 400 mls., (hi-lo-hi mission), 775 mls., (lo-lo-lo mission with external fuel), 530 mls., (hi-lo-hi mission with external fuel), 1,025 mls.; ferry range (maximum external fuel), 2,800 mls.

Weights: Normal loaded, 22,046 lb.; maximum, 29,762 lb.

Armament: Two 30-mm. (A) Aden or (S) DEFA cannon, and various external ordnance loads up to maximum (for short-range interdiction) of 10,000 lb.

Status: In production. First of seven prototypes flown September 8, 1968. Production contracts for 200 each for France and the U.K., and scheduled to enter service with *Armée de l'Air* in 1971 and R.A.F. in 1972.

Notes: Being developed jointly in France and the U.K. by the Société Européenne de Production de l'Avion Ecole de Combat et d'Appui Tactique (SEPECAT), the Jaguar is being developed in single-seat strike and two-seat trainer (illustrated) versions.

SEPECAT JAGUAR

Dimensions: Span, 27 ft. $10\frac{1}{3}$ in.; length, 53 ft. $10\frac{1}{2}$ in.;
height, 14 ft. $8\frac{1}{4}$ in.; wing area, 258·33 sq. ft.

SHIN MEIWA PS-1

Country of Origin: Japan.

Type: Long-range Maritime Patrol Flying Boat.

Power Plants: Four General Electric T64-IHI-10 turboprops each rated at 2,850 e.s.h.p.

Performance: Maximum speed, 340 m.p.h.; normal cruising speed, 196 m.p.h. at 4,920 ft.; initial climb rate, 2,264 ft./min.; maximum ceiling, 29,530 ft.; normal range, 1,347 mls.; maximum range, 2,948 mls.

Weights: Operational empty, 51,852 lb.; maximum loaded weight, 86,862 lb.

Armament: Maximum of four 2,165-lb. homing torpedoes, six 5-in. HVAR missiles, or four 330-lb. depth bombs.

Status: First prototype flown November 6, 1967, and second on June 14, 1968. Two pre-production and 20 production PS-1 flying boats to be manufactured for the Maritime Self-Defence Force with pre-production examples being delivered 1970 and production deliveries commencing 1971.

Notes: The PS-1 (formerly PX-S) employs an airscrew slipstream deflection system and boundary-layer control, a 1,250 s.h.p. T58-IHI-8B turboshaft being carried for the latter. The high length-to-beam ratio is claimed to provide exceptional seaworthiness, a groove-type spray suppressor evolved by the designer of the flying boat, Dr. Kikuhara, aiding operation in rough seas. The PS-1 has a normal crew complement of 12 members, and three six-aircraft squadrons are to be formed on this type.

SHIN MEIWA PS-1

Dimensions: Span, 107 ft. 7⅓ in.; length, 109 ft. 10¾ in.; height, 31 ft. 9¾ in.; wing area, 1,453·13 sq. ft.

SHORT SC.5/10 BELFAST C. MK. 1

Country of Origin: United Kingdom.
Type: Military Strategic Transport.
Power Plants: Four Rolls-Royce Tyne R.Ty.12 Mk. 101 turboprops each rated at 5,730 e.h.p.
Performance: Maximum cruising speed (at 200,000 lb.) 338 m.p.h. at 28,000 ft.; long-range cruising speed, 315 m.p.h. at 24,000 ft.; initial climb rate, 1,060 ft./min.; service ceiling, 30,000 ft.; range (30,000-lb. payload), 3,985 mls., (with max payload—80,000 lb.), 1,000 mls. at 315 m.p.h. at 25,000 ft.
Weights: Basic operational, 127,000 lb.; maximum loaded, 230,000 lb.
Accommodation: Flight crew of four plus air quartermaster. Typical military loads include three Alvis Saladin armoured cars, two Polaris-type missiles, three Wessex or four Whirlwind helicopters, or up to 80,000 lb. of freight for short-range tactical operations and 30,000 lb. in the strategic role.
Status: Production completed. First aircraft flown January 5, 1964, and 10th and last example late 1966.
Notes: Drag-reduction modifications on initial five aircraft delayed service introduction, but full-scale operation by No. 53 Squadron of the R.A.F.'s Air Support Command with part modified aircraft began in 1967, and delivery of fully modified aircraft began May 1968, modifications to all 10 aircraft being scheduled for completion in 1969.

SHORT SC.5/10 BELFAST C. MK. 1

Dimensions: Span, 158 ft. 9½ in.; length, 136 ft. 5 in.; height, 47 ft. 0 in.; wing area, 2,466 sq. ft.

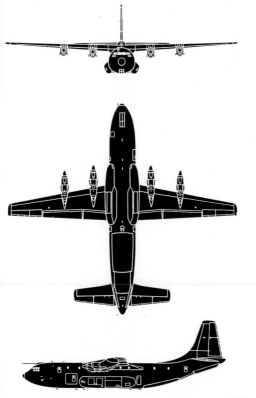

SHORT SKYVAN SERIES 3

Country of Origin: United Kingdom.

Type: Light Commercial Utility Transport.

Power Plants: Two Garrett AiResearch TPE 331-2-201A turboprops each rated at 755 e.s.h.p.

Performance: Maximum cruising speed, 200 m.p.h. at 10,000 ft.; long-range cruising speed, 170 m.p.h. at 10,000 ft.; range with maximum payload (4,600 lb.), 190 mls.; range with maximum fuel (and 2,894-lb. payload), 777 mls.; initial climb rate, 1,500 ft./min.; service ceiling (at 12,500 lb.), 21,000 ft.

Weights: Operational empty (freighter), 7,100 lb.; maximum loaded, 12,500 lb.

Accommodation: Flight crew of two with maximum of 18 passengers, or 12 casualty stretchers and two medical attendants.

Status: In production. First Skyvan Srs. 3 (conversion of third Srs. 2) flown December 15, 1967, and customer deliveries commenced summer 1968. Production rate of four per month was scheduled to be attained by beginning of 1969.

Notes: The Srs. 3 has supplanted the Srs. 2 owing to the failure of the Turboméca Astazou XII engines of the latter to meet specified performance. Only eight Astazou-powered Srs. 2 aircraft were delivered, and production of this model has been abandoned.

208

SHORT SKYVAN SERIES 3

Dimensions: Span, 63 ft. 11 in.; length, 40 ft. 1 in.; height, 15 ft. 1 in.; wing area, 373 sq. ft.

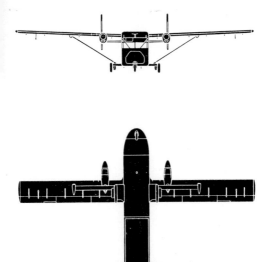

SIAI-MARCHETTI-FFA AS.202 BRAVO

Countries of Origin: Italy and Switzerland.
Type: Light Cabin Monoplane.
Power Plant: One Lycoming (AS.202-10) O-235-C1B or (AS.202-15) O-320-A2B four-cylinder horizontally-opposed engine rated at 115 and 150 h.p. respectively.
Performance: (Specification relates to AS.202-10 with figures in parentheses relating to AS-202-15) Maximum speed, 129 (143) m.p.h. at sea level; cruising speed at 75% power, 116 (133) m.p.h.; maximum range, 550 (528) mls.; initial climb rate, 708 (1,122) ft./min.; service ceiling, 13,120 (18,045) ft.
Weights: Empty, 1,135 (1,180) lb.; loaded, 1,764 (1,984) lb.
Accommodation: Two persons side by side with dual controls, and (AS.202-15) an optional third seat aft.
Status: Two prototypes under construction, both scheduled to commence flight testing early 1969. SIAI-Marchetti is also building three pre-series aircraft and envisages a production rate of eight per month for 1970. Current plans envisage separate assembly lines in Italy and Switzerland.
Notes: The Bravo is being developed jointly by the SIAI-Marchetti S.p.A. in Italy and the Flug-und Fahrzeugwerke A.G. in Switzerland. Apart from power plants, the two versions of the Bravo currently proposed are essentially similar, and will be fully aerobatic. Each of the participating companies is building a single prototype, and both factories will build complete aircraft.

SIAI-MARCHETTI-FFA AS.202 BRAVO

Dimensions: Span, 31 ft. 2 in.; length, 21 ft. 10 in.; height, 8 ft. 3 in.; wing area, 141·53 sq. ft.

SIAI-MARCHETTI S.208

Country of Origin: Italy
Type: Light Cabin Monoplane.
Power Plant: One Lycoming O-540-E4A5 six-cylinder horizontally-opposed engine rated at 260 h.p.
Performance: Maximum speed, 199 m.p.h. at sea level; cruising speed (75% power), 187 m.p.h. at 6,500 ft., (65% power), 176 m.p.h. at 8,200 ft.; service ceiling, 21,000 ft.; maximum range, 746 mls.
Weights: Empty, 1,720 lb.; loaded, 2,976 lb.
Accommodation: Basic accommodation for four persons in two pairs of side-by-side seats, with a collapsible seat installed in the baggage compartment for a fifth person.
Status: Prototype flown May 22, 1967. Initial series of 50 aircraft begun mid-1967. Production rate four–five per month, with first customer delivery early 1968.
Notes: The S.208 has been based on the lower-powered S.205 (see 1967 edition) and features individual rear seats in place of the bench of the earlier model, an optional fifth seat on which there are no weight restrictions, a third window on each side of the fuselage, electrical elevator trimming and electrically-operated flaps. Wingtip tanks are an optional extra which increase maximum range to 1,220 miles. The S.208 is being marketed in the U.S.A. with a 250 h.p. Franklin 6AS-350A engine as the Waco TS250-5 Vega, and 24 S.208s have been ordered by the Italian Air Force for training and liaison tasks.

212

SIAI-MARCHETTI S.208

Dimensions: Span, 35 ft. 7¾ in.; length, 27 ft. 2¾ in.; height, 9 ft. 5¾ in.; wing area, 173·19 sq. ft.

SIAI-MARCHETTI S.210

Country of Origin: Italy.
Type: Light Cabin Monoplane.
Power Plants: Two Lycoming TIO-360-A1B six-cylinder horizontally-opposed engines each rated at 200 h.p.
Performance: (Estimated) Maximum speed, 222 m.p.h. at sea level; maximum cruising speed, 211 m.p.h. at 8,000 ft.; economical cruising speed, 195 m.p.h. at 8,000 ft.; range (with maximum payload), 1,180 mls.; initial climb rate, 1,180 ft./min.; service ceiling, 26,500 ft.
Weights: Empty equipped, 2,271 lb.; maximum loaded, 4,078 lb.
Accommodation: Pilot and five passengers in three pairs of side-by-side seats.
Status: First prototype was scheduled to fly February 1969. Second prototype, one static test specimen, three pre-series and 20 production aircraft in hand at beginning of 1969.
Notes: The S.210 is a derivative of the single-engined S.205 series of light aircraft, and is intended to embody a number of the structural components of the latter. A prototype was originally scheduled to fly before the end of 1967, but SIAI-Marchetti gave priority to launching and establishing the company's single-engined line of cabin monoplanes.

SIAI-MARCHETTI S.210

Dimensions: Span, 38 ft. 2 in.; length, 28 ft. 2½ in.;
height, 10 ft. 1¼ in.; wing area, 185·5 sq. ft.

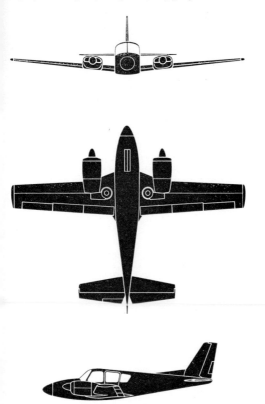

SIAI-MARCHETTI SF.260

Country of Origin: Italy

Type: Light Cabin Monoplane.

Power Plant: One Lycoming O-540-E4A5 six-cylinder horizontally-opposed engine rated at 260 h.p.

Performance: Maximum speed, 230 m.p.h. at sea level; cruising speed (75% power), 222 m.p.h. at 6,500 ft., (65% power), 210 m.p.h. at 8,200 ft.; initial climb rate, 1,770 ft./min.; service ceiling, 21,370 ft.; range, 1,050 mls.

Weights: Empty, 1,488 lb.; loaded (aerobatic), 2,200 lb., (utility), 2,425 lb.

Accommodation: Three persons in two side-by-side front seats and one person at rear.

Status: In production. Twenty-five delivered by beginning of 1969 when production rate was four per month on second batch (of 50) airframes.

Notes: The prototype, known as the F.250 and powered by a 250 h.p. Lycoming O-540-A1D, was flown July 15, 1964, and was built by Aviamilano. The second prototype, built by SIAI-Marchetti and powered by an up-rated engine, was designated SF.260 and appeared in 1966. The SF.260 is fully aerobatic with two persons and up to a gross weight of 2,200 lb. The SF.260 is marketed in the U.S.A. by Waco Aircraft as the SF260-3 Meteor 1 and, with a 250 h.p. Franklin 6AS-350A engine, as the TS250-3F Meteor 2.

216

SIAI-MARCHETTI SF.260

Dimensions: Span, 26 ft. 11¾ in.; length, 23 ft. 0 in.; height, 8 ft. 6 in.; wing area, 108·5 sq. ft.

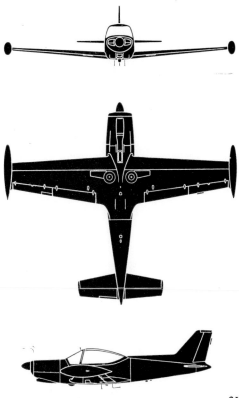

SIAT 223 FLAMINGO

Country of Origin: Federal Germany.

Type: Light Aerobatic Training (223K) and Touring (223N) Cabin Monoplane.

Power Plant: One Lycoming IO-360-C1A four-cylinder horizontally-opposed engine rated at 200 h.p.

Performance: (Specification relates to 223K with figures in parentheses relating to 223N) Maximum speed, 158 (155) m.p.h. at sea level; cruising speed at 75% power, 152 (149) m.p.h.; maximum range, (840) mls.; initial climb rate, 1,140 (827) ft./min.; service ceiling, 15,750 (13,780) ft.

Weights: Empty, 1,500 (1,545) lb.; maximum loaded, 1,985 (2,707) lb.

Accommodation: (223K) Two seats side by side, or (223N) four seats in two pairs.

Status: In production. First of four prototypes flown March 1, 1967, and production deliveries commencing in 1968.

Notes: Manufactured by the Bölkow subsidiary, Siebelwerke ATG, the Flamingo is being produced in two versions, the SIAT 223K aerobatic two-seater, and the enlarged SIAT 223N four-seat tourer. Purchasers include the Swissair-operated Swiss Air Transport School, which has acquired three 223Ks and seven 223Ns, and the Turkish state flying training organisation which has placed an initial contract for 15 and taken an option on a further 30.

218

SIAT 223 FLAMINGO

Dimensions: Span, 26 ft. 10¾ in. (30 ft. 10 in.); length, 24 ft. 4½ in. (26 ft. 4 in.); height, 8 ft. 2⅓ in.; wing area, 123·8 (140) sq. ft.

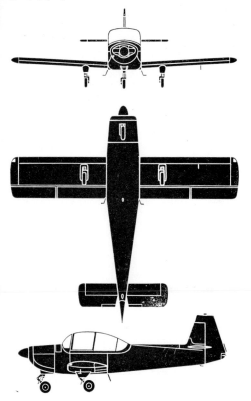

TED SMITH AEROSTAR MODEL 600

Country of Origin: U.S.A.
Type: Light Cabin Monoplane.
Power Plants: Two Lycoming IO-540-E1A5 six-cylinder horizontally-opposed engines each rated at 290 h.p.
Performance: Maximum speed, 260 m.p.h. at sea level; cruising speed at 10,000 ft. (70% power), 250 m.p.h. (65% power), 240 m.p.h., (55% power), 225 m.p.h.; range (with 30 min. reserves), 1,400 mls. at 240 m.p.h. at 10,000 ft.; initial climb rate, 1,850 ft./min.; service ceiling, 22,000 ft.
Weights: Empty equipped, 3,425 lb.; maximum loaded, 5,500 lb.
Accommodation: Six persons in paired individual seats, and 240-lb. capacity luggage compartment.
Status: In production. Prototype Model 600 flown December 20, 1967, with first production aircraft following in May 1968, and first production deliveries in October 1968.
Notes: The Model 600 is the first production version of the basic Aerostar design, and has been joined by the Model 601, the first example of which flew on July 9, 1968, and the Model 620. The Model 601 differs from the Model 600 described and illustrated in having turbo-supercharged TIO-540 engines of 310 h.p., and the Model 620, which will have TIO-541-A1A engines of a similar rating, is a pressurised version. The last-mentioned model is expected to fly in 1969.

TED SMITH AEROSTAR MODEL 600

Dimensions: Span, 34 ft. 2½ in.; length, 34 ft. 10 in.; height, 12 ft. 1 in.; wing area, 170 sq. ft.

SOCATA ST 10 PROVENCE

Country of Origin: France.
Type: Light Cabin Monoplane.
Power Plant: One Lycoming IO-360-C four-cylinder horizontally-opposed engine rated at 200 h.p.
Performance: Maximum speed, 180 m.p.h. at sea level; cruising speed (70% power), 168 m.p.h.; range (with maximum payload), 810 mls.
Weights: Empty equipped, 1,499 lb.; maximum loaded, 2,623 lb.
Accommodation: Pilot and three passengers in pairs, Dual controls fitted as standard and baggage space of 88-lb. capacity aft of rear seats.
Status: In production. Prototype flown (as Super Horizon 200) on November 7, 1967. Production deliveries scheduled to commence early 1969.
Notes: The Provence has been developed from the GY 80 Horizon by SOCATA (Société de Construction d'Avions de Tourisme et d'Affaires), a division of Sud-Aviation. The Provence retains the wing and basically similar tail surfaces to those of the Horizon, but marries these components to an entirely redesigned and aerodynamically-refined fuselage and a more powerful engine. Like its predecessor, the Provence possesses an essentially similar all-metal structure. A manufacturing licence for both the Horizon and Provence has been acquired by Southern Aeronautics of Perth, Australia.

222

SOCATA ST 10 PROVENCE

Dimensions: Span, 31 ft. 9¾ in.; length, 22 ft. 4⅛ in.; height, 8 ft. 4⅜ in.; wing area, 139·93 sq. ft.

SOKO JASTREB

Country of Origin: Yugoslavia.
Type: Single-seat Light Tactical Strike and Reconnaissance aircraft.
Power Plant: One Rolls-Royce Bristol Viper 531 turbojet rated at 3,130 lb.s.t.
Performance: Maximum speed, 510 m.p.h. at 19,680 ft.; maximum cruising speed, 460 m.p.h. at 16,400 ft.; initial climb rate, 4,135 ft./min.; service ceiling, 39,375 ft.; maximum range, 945 miles at 29,520 ft.
Weights: Empty equipped (Jastreb-1) 5,753 lb., (Jastreb-2) 5,996 lb.; loaded without external stores (Jastreb-1) 8,748 lb., (Jastreb-2) 8,804 lb.; maximum loaded (Jastreb-1), 9,850 lb., (Jastreb-2), 9,350 lb.
Armament: (Jastreb-1) Three 12·7-mm. Colt-Browning machine guns with 135 r.p.g., plus two 551-lb. 220-lb., or 110-lb. bombs, or six 57-mm. or 127-mm. air-to-ground missiles.
Status: Prototypes flown in 1966 and production deliveries to the Yugoslav Air Force early 1969.
Notes: The Jastreb (Hawk) has been evolved from the Soko Galeb (Gull) tandem two-seat basic trainer from which it differs primarily in having a single cockpit with a sideways-hinged canopy, a more powerful Viper turbojet, and some structural strengthening. Two versions are in production, the Jastreb-1 light attack aircraft and the Jastreb-2 tactical reconnaissance aircraft.

SOKO JASTREB

Dimensions: Span, 34 ft. 8 in.; length, 35 ft. 1½ in.;
height, 11 ft. 11½ in.; wing area, 204·5 sq. ft.

SOKO KRAGUJ

Country of Origin: Yugoslavia.

Type: Single-seat Light Close-support and Counter-insurgency Aircraft.

Power Plant: One Lycoming GSO-480-B1A6 six-cylinder horizontally-opposed engine rated at 340 h.p.

Performance: Maximum speed, 171 m.p.h. at sea level, 183 m.p.h. at 4,920 ft.; maximum cruising speed, 174 m.p.h. at 4,920 ft.; initial climb rate, 1,340 ft./min.; maximum range, 497 miles.

Weights: Empty equipped, 2,491 lb.; maximum loaded, 3,580 lb.

Armament: Two 7·7-mm. machine guns with 650 r.p.g. plus two 220-lb. bombs, two 127-mm. air-to-ground missiles, two 33 Imp. gal. napalm tanks, or two 12-round rocket packs.

Status: Flown in prototype form in 1966, with production deliveries from Mostar commencing late 1968.

Notes: The Kraguj has been developed as an inexpensive light tactical aircraft capable of operation from unprepared grass strips, and suitable for a variety of roles, including close-support, reconnaissance, aerobatic and armament training, anti-helicopter missions, and light logistic support. The Kraguj is of all-metal construction, and design emphasis has been placed on structural simplicity and ease of maintenance in the field. It is envisaged that the Kraguj will equip second-line formations for operation in support of partisan-type activities.

226

SOKO KRAGUJ

Dimensions: Span, 34 ft. 9 in.; length, 25 ft. 11 in.;
height, 9 ft. 10 in.; wing area, 182·986 sq. ft.

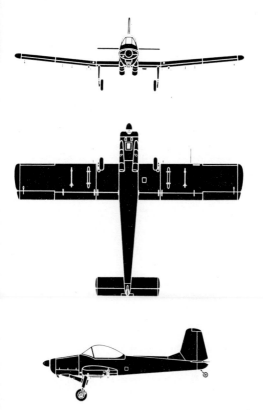

SUD-AVIATION CARAVELLE 11R

Country of Origin: France.

Type: Medium-range Commercial Passenger and Freight Transport.

Power Plants: Two Pratt & Whitney JT8D-7 turbofans each rated at 14,000 lb.s.t.

Performance: Maximum cruising speed, 498 m.p.h. at 24,600 ft., 490 m.p.h. at 27,430 ft.; range (with maximum payload—20,060 lb.), 1,430 mls.; (with 16,500-lb. payload), 1,760 mls.

Weight: Maximum loaded, 114,640 lb.

Accommodation: Mixed passenger-freight with provision for 50 tourist-class passengers in rear cabin plus 656·7 cu. ft. cargo space in forward cabin and 581 cu. ft. in cargo hold. In all-passenger configuration a maximum of 89 tourist-class passengers may be carried.

Status: In production. The production prototype of the Caravelle 11R commenced trials on April 21, 1967, with delivery (to Air-Afrique) following in summer 1967. First of two prototype Caravelles flown on May 27, 1955, first production aircraft following on May 18, 1958. Production programme currently covers 260 Caravelle-series aircraft of which 253 had been ordered by the beginning of 1969 when production rate was one aircraft per month.

Notes: Caravelle 11R is derivative of 10R with large freight-loading door, strengthened freight floor, and a 36·6-in. additional section in forward fuselage. The Caravelle 11R has been delivered to Air Afrique and Air Congo, and some 250 Caravelles of all types were in airline service by the beginning of 1969.

228

SUD-AVIATION CARAVELLE 11R

Dimensions: Span, 112 ft. 6½ in.; length 107 ft. 3¾ in.; height, 28 ft. 7½ in.; wing area, 1,579 sq. ft.

SUKHOI SU-7M (FITTER)

Country of Origin: U.S.S.R.
Type: Single-seat Ground Attack Fighter.
Power Plant: One axial-flow turbojet rated at approximately 15,500 lb.s.t. and 22,050 lb.s.t. with afterburning.
Performance: (Estimated) Maximum speed (without external stores), 1,056 m.p.h. at 36,000 ft. (Mach 1·6), (with two 132 Imp. gal. drop tanks and two rocket pods), 790 m.p.h. (Mach 1·2); initial climb rate (without external stores), 30,000 ft./min., (high drag configuration), 23,500 ft./min.
Weights: (Estimated) Loaded (clean), 27,000 lb.; maximum overload, 30,500 lb.
Armament: Four 550-lb. bombs on external pylors (two beneath fuselage and two under wings), or two 550-lb. bombs plus two pods each housing 19 55-mm. rockets. Two 30-mm. cannon in wing roots.
Status: In production. Prototype allegedly flown 1955 and first production deliveries 1958–59.
Notes: The Su-7M is currently standard ground attack fighter equipment with the Soviet, Czech, Polish and Egyptian air arms, and entered service with the Indian Air Force during the course of 1968. A tandem two-seat training version, the Su-7UTI (Moujik), is also in service. The Su-7 was evolved in parallel with Su-9 (Fishpot) all-weather delta interceptor, the two aircraft employing similar fuselages and tail surfaces married to wings optimised for the specific role of each model. A version intended primarily for soft-field operation is designated Su-7BKL in Czech service.

230

SUKHOI SU-7M (FITTER)

Dimensions: (Estimated) Span, 32 ft. 3 in.; length,
55 ft. 0 in.; height, 16 ft. 0 in.

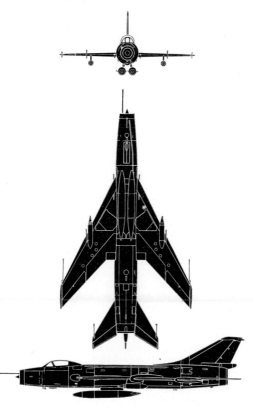

SUKHOI SU-9 (FISHPOT)

Country of Origin: U.S.S.R.
Type: Single-seat All-weather Interceptor Fighter.
Power Plant: One axial-flow turbojet of 15,500 (approx.) lb.s.t. and 22,050 (approx.) lb.s.t. with afterburning.
Performance: (Estimated) Maximum speed without external stores, 1,190 m.p.h. at 40,000 ft. (Mach 1·8), with two Anab or four Alkali AAMs 990 m.p.h. (Mach 1·5); normal cruising speed, 570–600 m.p.h. at 36,000–40,000 ft.; initial climb rate, 27,000 ft./min.; time to 40,000 ft., 4·5 min.; service ceiling, 55,000 ft.
Weights: (Estimated) Loaded (clean), 25,500 lb.; maximum loaded, 29,000–30,000 lb.
Armament: Four Alkali or two Anab AAMs on underwing pylons.
Status: In production. Prototype of developed version illustrated was demonstrated publicly in 1961 and is believed to have supplanted earlier variants from 1965.
Notes: The Su-9 originally possessed some component commonality with the Su-7 (see pages 230–1), the fuselages and tail assemblies of the two aircraft being similar. The latest service variant of this single-seat interceptor as demonstrated at Domododovo on July 9, 1967, features an enlarged air intake, and the nose centre-body had been enlarged and moved forward to produce a two-shock intake. The Su-9 is illustrated with two 132 (approx.) Imp. gal. drop tanks beneath the fuselage.

SUKHOI SU-9 (FISHPOT)

Estimated Dimensions: Span, 31 ft. 0 in.; length, 55 ft. 0 in.; height, 16 ft. 0 in., wing area, 425 sq. ft.

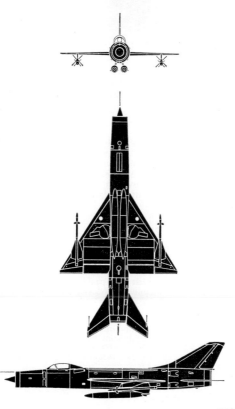

SUKHOI SU-11 (?) FLAGON-A

Country of Origin: U.S.S.R.

Type: Single-seat Interceptor Fighter.

Power Plants: Two turbojets each rated at approximately 15,500 lb.s.t. and 22,050 lb.s.t. with afterburning.

Performance: (Estimated) Maximum speed, 1,850 m.p.h. at 40,000 ft. (Mach 2·8), 910 m.p.h. at sea level (Mach 1·2).

Weights: Approximate loaded, 50,000–55,000 lb.

Armament: Two air-to-air missiles on underwing pylons, possibly of Anab type.

Status: In production. Believed first entered operational service with Soviet Air Force in 1968.

Notes: Presumably intended as a successor to the Su-9 and possibly designated Su-11, this twin-jet all-weather interceptor may be considered as, in effect, an enlarged and considerably refined development of the Su-9, much of the design of the earlier aircraft, including the cockpit enclosure, undercarriage, delta wing, airbrake location and vertical rail, being retained. A short-take-off-and-landing version of the basic design (illustrated in the 1968 edition and dubbed Flagon-B) features two direct lift engines installed in the fuselage ahead of the propulsion units, two aft-hinged doors for these being provided in the upper fuselage decking, the exhaust outlets being covered by folding doors. In addition to the lift engine installation, the STOL version features extended outboard wing panels which, of reduced leading-edge sweep, result in a double-delta configuration.

234

SUKHOI SU-11 (?) FLAGON-A

Estimated Dimensions: Span, 33 ft. 6 in., length, 71 ft.
o in.; height, 16 ft. o in.

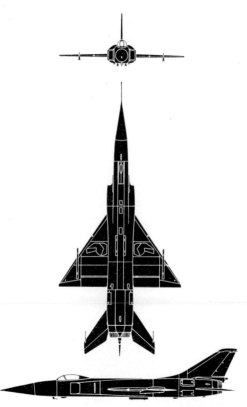

SWEARINGEN MERLIN IIB

Country of Origin: U.S.A.

Type: Light Executive Transport.

Power Plants: Two Garrett–AiResearch TPE331-1-151G turboprops each rated at 665 s.h.p.

Performance: Cruising speed, 295 m.p.h. at 15,000 ft.; maximum range, 1,785 mls. at 272 m.p.h. at 27,500 ft. with 45 min. reserves; initial climb rate, 2,570 ft./min.; service ceiling, 29,900 ft.

Weights: Empty equipped, 6,450 lb.; maximum loaded, 10,000 lb.

Accommodation: Crew of two on flight deck with dual controls, and standard accommodation for six passengers in main cabin.

Status: In production. Prototype Merlin flown April 13, 1965, and deliveries of initial model (Merlin IIA) began August 26, 1966. Thirty-six Merlin IIAs manufactured when type supplanted by Merlin IIB of which deliveries commenced September 1968 with 40 scheduled for delivery by beginning of 1969 when production was to have attained four per month.

Notes: Merlin IIB differs from IIA (550 s.h.p. PT6A-20 turboprops) in power plants and pressurisation system, and mates modified Beechcraft Queen Air wings and Twin Bonanza undercarriage with a completely new pressurised fuselage. Merlin IIA may be re-engined with 615 s.h.p. PT6A-27 engines.

236

SWEARINGEN MERLIN IIB

Dimensions: Span, 45 ft. 11 in.; length, 40 ft. 1¼ in.; height, 14 ft. 1 in.; wing area, 279·7 sq. ft.

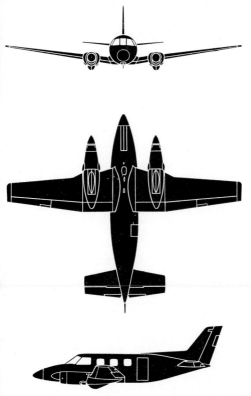

SWEARINGEN METRO

Country of Origin: U.S.A.

Type: Light Commercial Feederliner.

Power Plants: Two Garrett–AiResearch TPE331-303 turboprops each rated at 895 e.s.h.p.

Performance: (Estimated) Maximum cruising speed, 300 m.p.h. at 20,000 ft.; range (with 4,350-lb. payload), 115 mls. at 248 m.p.h. at 10,000 ft., (with 3,900-lb. payload), 460 mls. at 245 m.p.h. at 10,000 ft., (with 2,000-lb. payload), 1,380 mls. at 253 m.p.h. at 20,000 ft.; maximum cruising altitude, 25,000 ft.

Weights: Manufacturer's empty, 7,000 lb.; empty equipped, 7,500 lb.; maximum loaded, 12,500 lb.

Accommodation: Flight crew of two with maximum of 20 passengers. Quick change features for conversion to freight or freight-and-passenger configuration include removable seats and a movable bulkhead.

Status: Prototype scheduled to commence flight testing in May 1969 with FAA certification early 1970 when production deliveries will commence.

Notes: The Metro third-level-type or commuter airliner is to be marketed jointly by Swearingen and Fairchild Hiller, and the latter company is also expected to manufacture Metro components under subcontract. The Metro is claimed to offer exceptionally good field performance, taking-off within 3,000 ft. at 12,500 lb.

238

SWEARINGEN METRO

Dimensions: Span, 46 ft. 3 in.; length, 58 ft. 0 in.; height, 17 ft. 0⅓ in.; wing area, 277·5 sq. ft.

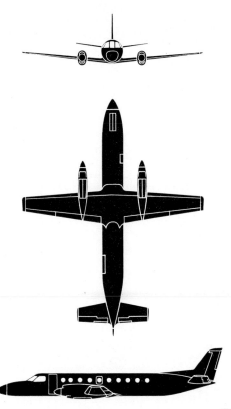

TRANSALL C.160

Country of Origin: France and Germany.
Type: Medium-range Tactical Transport.
Power Plants: Two Rolls-Royce Tyne R.Ty.20 Mk. 22 turboprops each rated at 5,665 s.h.p. (6,100 e.s.h.p.).
Performance: Maximum cruising speed (at 90,390 lb.), 332 m.p.h. at 14,800 ft.; economical cruising speed, 308 m.p.h. at 26,250 ft.; service ceiling, 27,900 ft.; range (with maximum payload—35,280 lb., and 10% reserves plus 30 min.), 1,070 mls., (with maximum fuel and 17,640-lb. payload), 3,010 mls.
Weights: Operational empty, 61,843 lb.; normal loaded, 97,440 lb.; maximum, 108,250 lb.
Accommodation: Crew of four and 81 troops or 62 casualty stretchers and four medical attendants. Other possible loads include armoured vehicles, tanks and tractors not exceeding 35,270 lb. weight.
Status: In production. First of three prototypes flown February 25, 1963, and first of six pre-production aircraft on May 21, 1965. Current orders call for 160 production aircraft (50 C.160Fs for France and 110 C.160Ds for Federal Germany) of which first completed May 17, 1967. Production rate is three per month with VFW and HFB in Germany assembling 54 and 53 respectively, and Nord-Aviation in France assembling 53, current orders scheduled to be completed in 1972.
Notes: Joint Franco–German programme. Order for nine for South Africa negotiated 1966 for 1969 delivery.

TRANSALL C.160

Dimensions: Span, 131 ft. 2½ in.; length, 105 ft. 3½ in.;
height, 38 ft. 4¾ in.; wing area, 1,722·7 sq. ft.

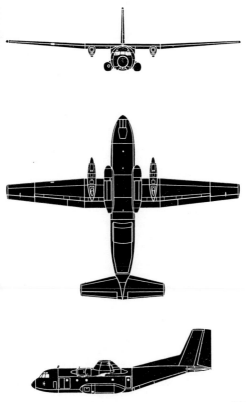

TUPOLEV TU-22 (BLINDER-B)

Country of Origin: U.S.S.R.

Type: Long-range Medium Bomber and Strike-reconnaissance aircraft.

Power Plants: Two turbojets rated at approximately 20,000 lb.s.t. and 27,000 lb.s.t. with afterburning.

Performance: (Estimated) Maximum speed, 990 m.p.h. at 40,000 ft. (Mach 1·5); maximum cruising speed, 630 m.p.h. at 40,000 ft.; unrefuelled tactical radius, 1,400 mls.; maximum range, 4,000 mls.; service ceiling 60,000 ft.

Weights: Approximate loaded, 185,000 lb.

Armament: Free-falling weapons housed internally, or single semi-recessed Kitchen stand-off missile. Defensive: Single 23-mm. cannon in remotely controlled tail barbette.

Status: In production. Believed to have attained operational status with the Soviet Air Force in 1965, and with shore-based elements of the Soviet naval arm in 1967.

Notes: Successor to the subsonic Tu-16 (Badger) the Tu-22 was originally evolved by the Tupolev design bureau in the mid-'fifties as the *Samolet* "Yu" with the design bureau designation Tu-105. The most recent examples of the Tu-22 seen embody a number of modifications, these including an extended flight refuelling probe and enlarged engine air intakes nacelles and exhaust orifices. Camera windows are provided in the nose and aft, the standard crew complement comprises four members, and the tail gun is presumably intended to dispense a mixture of "chaff" and tracer. A training version with a raised second cockpit for the instructor is in service.

TUPOLEV TU-22 (BLINDER-B)

Estimated Dimensions: Span, 91 ft. 0 in.; length 133 ft. 0 in.; height, 17 ft. 0 in.; wing area, 2,030 sq. ft.

TUPOLEV TU-134A (CRUSTY)

Country of Origin: U.S.S.R.

Type: Short- and Medium-range Commercial Transport.

Power Plants: Two Soloviev D-30 turbofans each rated at 14,990 lb.s.t.

Performance: Maximum cruising speed, 572 m.p.h. economical cruising speed, 528 m.p.h. at 32,810 ft. range (with 15,432-lb. payload and one hour reserves at 88,185 lb.), 777 mls., (at 97,000 lb.), 1,490 mls. (with 11,023-lb. payload at 88,185 lb.), 1,180 mls. (at 97,000 lb.), 1,926 mls.

Weights: Empty equipped, 56,218 lb.; normal loaded 88,185 lb.; maximum loaded, 97,000 lb.

Accommodation: Normal flight crew of three. Two basic cabin arrangements, one accommodating 16 first-class and 48 tourist-class passengers, and the other 72 tourist-class passengers.

Status: In production. Prototype flown in second half of 1962. Five pre-production aircraft produced 1963-1964. First production deliveries (to Aeroflot) in 1966 and entered service in 1967.

Notes: Derived directly from the Tu-124 (and originally known as the Tu-124A), the Tu-134A has a similar fuselage cross-section to that of its predecessor, but there are now few common components between the two aircraft types. The Tu-134A employs a similar system of double-slotted flaps and air brakes to that of the Tu-124.

244

TUPOLEV TU-134A (CRUSTY)

Dimensions: Span, 95 ft. 2 in.; length, 114 ft. 10 in.; height, 29 ft. 7 in.; wing area, 1,370·3 sq. ft.

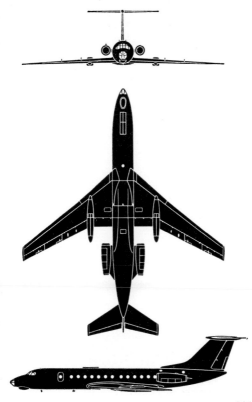

TUPOLEV TU-144

Country of Origin: U.S.S.R.

Type: Long-haul Supersonic Commercial Transport.

Power Plants: Four Kuznetsov NK-144 turbofans each rated at 28,660 lb.s.t. and 38,580 lb.s.t. with afterburning.

Performance: (Estimated) Maximum cruising speed, 1,550 m.p.h. at 49,200–65,600 ft. (Mach 2·35); service ceiling, 65,600 ft.; maximum ceiling, 68,900 ft.; maximum range, 4,040 mls.

Weights: Maximum loaded, 330,000 lb.

Accommodation: Basic flight crew of three and standard layout for 100 passengers in two cabins (forward cabin accommodating 18 passengers in three-abreast seating and aft cabin accommodating 82 in five- and four-abreast seating). Alternative layouts for 108 and 121 passengers.

Status: Prototype development. Two flying prototypes and one static test specimen to be followed by four pre-production examples. First prototype flown December 31, 1968, and service introduction by Aeroflot scheduled for 1971.

Notes: The world's first supersonic transport to fly, and designed to operate at similar speeds to those of the Anglo-French Concorde, the Tu-144 is claimed to be capable of operating at costs matching those of contemporary long-haul subsonic transports. Like the Concorde, it employs an ogival delta wing, and a droopable nose for take-off and landing. The main undercarriage members each comprise 12-wheel bogies.

TUPOLEV TU-144

Dimensions: (Estimated) Span, 81 ft. 0 in.; length,
180 ft. 0 in.; height, 37 ft. 0 in.

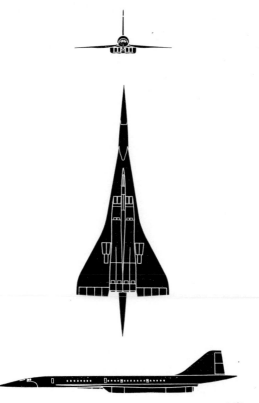

TUPOLEV TU-154

Country of Origin: U.S.S.R.

Type: Medium-range Commercial Transport.

Power Plants: Three Kuznetsov NK-8-2 turbofans each rated at 20,940 lb.s.t.

Performance: (Estimated) Maximum cruising speed, 564 m.p.h. at 39,370 ft.; economical cruising speed, 484 m.p.h.; range (with 35,840-lb. payload and 1 hr. reserves), 2,100 mls. at 550 m.p.h. at 36,000 ft., (with 23,520-lb. payload), 3,730 mls.; take-off distance (at 173,063 lb. to clear 50 ft.), 4,380 ft., (at 187,393 lb.), 4,920 ft.; landing distance (at 134,400 lb. from 50 ft.), 4,760 ft., (at 147,840 lb.), 5,100 ft.

Weights: Empty, 88,626 lb.; max. loaded (initial), 176,370 lb., (definitive), 189,598 lb.

Accommodation: Three crew members and 152 tourist-class passengers. Alternative versions provide accommodation for 164 economy-class passengers or 24 tourist- and 104 economy-class passengers. A proposed freighter variant will carry up to 56,000 lb. of cargo.

Status: Under development. First prototype flown October 4, 1968, with first deliveries to Aeroflot scheduled for 1970.

Notes: Intended as a successor to the Tu-104 in Aeroflot service, the Tu-154 is expected to commence route flying late 1968. Proposals call for a stretched version, the Tu-154M, accommodating 250 passengers and having uprated NK-8 turbofans for service from 1972–73.

248

TUPOLEV TU-154

Dimensions: Span, 123 ft. 2⅓ in.; length, 157 ft. 1¾ in.; height, 37 ft. 4¾ in.; wing area, 2,168·92 sq. ft.

VFW-FIAT VAK 191B

Countries of Origin: Federal Germany and Italy.
Type: Single-seat V/STOL Strike Fighter.
Power Plants: One Rolls-Royce/MAN Turbo RB.193-12 vectored thrust turbofan rated at 10,150 lb.s.t., and (lift) two Rolls-Royce RB.162-81 turbojets each rated at 5,568 lb.s.t.
Performance: (Estimated) Maximum speed, 730 m.p.h. (Mach 0·96) at 1,000 ft., 605 m.p.h. (Mach 0·92) at 40,000 ft.; tactical radius (lo-lo-lo mission with full internal weapons load), 230 mls. at 610 m.p.h. (Mach 0·8).
Weights: Empty, 10,100 lb.; maximum loaded (for vertical take-off), 17,600 lb., (short take-off), 19,400 lb.
Armament: Internal bay for interchangeable packs containing two 30-mm. cannon and ammunition, retractable rocket launchers, bombs, reconnaissance equipment, or auxiliary fuel. Up to six weapons attachment points may be provided on the fuselage and a further four beneath the wings.
Status: Six prototypes under construction with work being shared equally between the Vereinigte Flugtechnische Werk (VFW) in Germany and Fiat in Italy. First prototype scheduled for completion mid-1969 with flight tests commencing October–November 1969, and all six flying by 1971.
Notes: As a result of changes in German strategy, the VAK 191B programme is now considered purely experimental and will proceed no further than prototype evaluation.

250

VFW-FIAT VAK 191B

Dimensions: Span, 18 ft. 4⅓ in.; length, 48 ft. 3½ in.; height, 14 ft. 0¾ in.; wing area, 134·5 sq. ft.

YAKOVLEV YAK-40 (CODLING)

Country of Origin: U.S.S.R.

Type: Short-haul Commercial Transport.

Power Plants: Three Ivchenko AI-25 turbofans each rated at 3,307 lb.s.t.

Performance: Maximum speed, 435 m.p.h.; maximum cruising speed, 373 m.p.h.; normal cruising speed, 342 m.p.h.; long-range cruising speed, 310 m.p.h.; range (with 6,150-lb. payload and 45 min. reserves), 373 mls., (with maximum fuel and 3,593-lb. payload), 900 mls.

Weights: Empty, 18,916 lb.; normal loaded, 27,392 lb.; maximum loaded, 29,210 lb.

Accommodation: Basic flight crew of two and basic layout for 24 passengers in three-abreast seating or high-density layout for maximum of 31 passengers.

Status: In production. First of five prototypes flown October 21, 1966, and first deliveries to Aeroflot commenced mid-1968.

Notes: Intended primarily as a successor to the Li-2 (licence-built DC-3) in Aeroflot service, the Yak-40 places accent on maintenance simplicity and short-field capability. All three engines are operated on take-off, but the central engine may be throttled back to idle for fuel economy during cruise. Retractable airstairs are provided in the rear fuselage, and for simplicity there is a single services hydraulic system which operates the undercarriage, airstairs, nosewheel steering, tailplane setting gear and flaps.

YAKOVLEV YAK-40 (CODLING)

Dimensions: Span, 82 ft. 0¼ in.; length, 66 ft. 3 in.; height, 20 ft. 11 in.; wing area, 753·473 sq. ft.

YAKOVLEV FREEHAND

Country of Origin: U.S.S.R.
Type: Single-seat Vertical Take-off and Landing Development Aircraft.
Power Plants: Two 7,000–9,000 lb.s.t. vectored-thrust turbofans.
Performance: Estimated maximum speed, 645 m.p.h. at sea level (Mach 0·85); maximum cruising speed, 500 m.p.h. at 5,000 ft. (Mach 0·8); tactical radius (VTOL), 100–150 mls. at sea level, (STOL), 150–200 mls.
Weights: Approximate max. (STOL), 18,000 lb.
Status: Believed experimental only. Possibly serving as basis for operational lightweight V/STOL strike and reconnaissance aircraft.
Notes: Publicly revealed at Domodedovo in July 1967 when two examples were seen, this vertical-take-off-and-landing aircraft has been attributed to the design bureau of Alexander Yakovlev, although its origin was not known with certainty at the time of closing for press. Of cropped-delta configuration with bicycle-type main undercarriage members and forward-retracting outrigger stabilising wheels, the aircraft has side-by-side turbofans exhausting through two swivelling nozzles at the centre of gravity. Stabilisation in hover is provided by four puffer pipes, one at each wingtip, one in the boom protruding from the nose, and one beneath the tail. It is to be assumed that in the case of failure of one turbofan the gas stream from the remaining powerplant can be ducted to both nozzles.

254

YAKOVLEV FREEHAND

Estimated Dimensions: Span, 27 ft. 0 in.; length (including 8 ft. nose boom), 53 ft. 0 in.; height, 13 ft. 0 in.

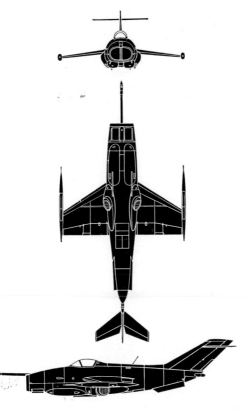

ZLIN Z 42

Country of Origin: Czechoslovakia.
Type: Light Cabin Monoplane.
Power Plant: One Walter M 137 six-cylinder inverted air-cooled engine rated at 180 h.p.
Performance: Maximum speed, 143 m.p.h. at sea level; maximum cruising speed, 133 m.p.h.; range (standard tankage), 497 mls., (long-range tankage), 808 mls.; initial climb rate, 984 ft./min.; service ceiling, 18,045 ft.
Weights: Empty, 1,312–1,378 lb.; loaded (aerobatics), 1,852 lb.; maximum, 2,028 lb.
Accommodation: Side-by-side seats for two persons with dual controls.
Status: Prototype flown for first time on October 17, 1967, and first production deliveries from Otrokovice are scheduled to commence in 1969.
Notes: Designed by Jan Mikula and built at the Moravan works at Otrokovice, the Z 42 is an all-metal, fully-aerobatic aircraft particularly suitable for training, and a four-seat version, the Z 43, is being developed simultaneously, and is expected to fly during 1969. The Z 43 possesses 80% commonality of structural components with the Z 42, and is to be powered by a 210 h.p. M 337 engine. The Z 43 will have a maximum loaded weight of 2,756 lb., and estimated performance includes a similar maximum speed to that of the Z 42, an initial climb rate of 650 ft./min., and a normal range of 466 miles.

ZLIN Z 42

Dimensions: Span, 27 ft. 10¾ in.; length, 23 ft. 2⅓ in.; wing area, 134·549 sq. ft.

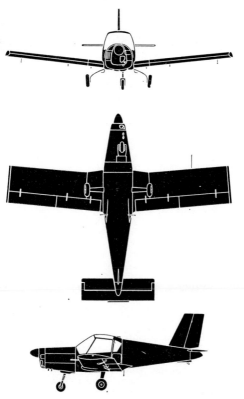

BELL (UH-1H) 205 IROQUOIS

Country of Origin: U.S.A.
Type: Utility and Transport Helicopter.
Power Plant: One Lycoming T53-L-13 turboshaft rated at 1,250 s.h.p.
Performance: Maximum speed (at 9,025 lb.), 138 m.p.h.; cruising speed, 136 m.p.h.; normal range (at 9,025 lb.), 327 mls.; maximum inclined climb rate, 1,760 ft./min.; hovering ceiling (in ground effect), 20,000 ft., (out of ground effect), 15,600 ft.
Weights: Empty, 4,850 lb.; normal loaded, 9,025 lb.
Dimensions: Rotor diameter, 48 ft. 0 in.; fuselage length, 42 ft. 0 in.; overall height, 14 ft. 6 in.
Notes: The UH-1H is the principal current production version of the Model 205 Iroquois utility helicopter, and is essentially similar to the UH-1D apart from having a T53-L-13 turboshaft in place of the T53-L-11 derated to 1,100 s.h.p. The UH-1H can accommodate 12 troops, six casualty litters and a medical attendant, or 4,000 lb. of freight, and 2,074 examples of this variant of the Iroquois had been ordered by the end of 1968. The UH-1D Iroquois is manufactured under licence in Italy and Federal Germany, and is distinguished from the earlier UH-1B primarily in providing greater cabin space. The Iroquois has been supplied to many air arms.

BELL (OH-58A) 206A JETRANGER

Country of Origin: U.S.A.
Type: Five-seat Utility Helicopter.
Power Plant: One Allison 250-C18 turboshaft rated at 317 s.h.p.
Performance: Maximum speed, 150 m.p.h., cruising speed (at 2,900 lb.), 134 m.p.h., maximum inclined climb rate, 1,600 ft./min., hovering ceiling (in ground effect), 8,800 ft., (out of ground effect), 4,200 ft., range 359 mls. at 137 m.p.h.
Weights: Empty, 1,295 lb.; loaded, 2,900 lb.
Dimensions: Rotor diameter, 33 ft. 4 in.; fuselage length, 28 ft. 2 in.; overall height, 9 ft. 6 in.
Notes: The JetRanger, the prototype of which was flown for the first time on January 10, 1966, is a derivative of Bell's unsuccessful original entry in the U.S. Army's LOH (Light Observation Helicopter) contest. Two additional prototypes have been used in the development programme, and the first production JetRanger deliveries were effected in January 1967. Lighter and faster than its LOH predecessor, the OH-4A, the JetRanger has a refined structure, and in a re-opened LOH contest in 1968, a contract was awarded by the U.S. Army for 2,200 JetRangers under the designation OH-58A. Forty have been delivered to U.S. Navy for training as TH-57As (illustrated).

BELL (AH-1G) 209 HUEYCOBRA

Country of Origin: U.S.A.
Type: Two-seat Attack Helicopter.
Power Plant: One Lycoming T53-L-13 turboshaft rated at 1,250 s.h.p.
Performance: Maximum speed (at 8,624 lb.), 186 m.p.h.; cruising speed, 166 m.p.h.; normal range (at 8,624 lb.), 425 mls.; maximum inclined climb rate (at 8,624 lb.), 1,900 ft./min.; hovering ceiling (in ground effect), 18,600 ft., (out of ground effect), 11,900 ft.
Weights: Empty, 5,510 lb.; normal loaded, 8,624 lb.
Dimensions: Rotor diameter, 44 ft. 0 in.; fuselage length, 44 ft. 4¾ in.; overall height, 13 ft. 7¼ in.
Armament: One TAT-102 nose turret with one 7·62-mm. GAU-2B/A Minigun with 8,000 rounds, plus four XM-159 packs of 19 70-mm. rockets, four XM-157 packs of seven 70-mm. rockets, two XM-18 gun pods each with one 7·62-mm. Minigun, or six TOW wire-guided missiles.
Notes: The Model 209, or AH-1G, is currently entering U.S. Army service, and a total of 838 helicopters of this type had been ordered by the end of November 1968. The TAT-102 nose turret is to be supplanted by XM-28 turret mounting a Minigun and an XM-129 40-mm. grenade launcher. The AH-1J is a U.S. Marine Corps version with PT6T "Twin Pac" power plant.
260

BOEING-VERTOL CH-47C CHINOOK

Country of Origin: U.S.A.

Type: Medium Tactical Transport Helicopter.

Power Plants: Two Lycoming T55-L-11 turboshafts each rated at 3,750 s.h.p.

Performance: Maximum speed, 184 m.p.h. at 5,000 ft.; maximum radius of action (at 33,000 lb.), 214 mls.; maximum inclined climb rate, 2,740 ft./min.; hovering ceiling (out of ground effect), 13,850 ft.; service ceiling, 19,500 ft.

Weights: Empty, 20,026 lb.; normal loaded, 33,000 lb.; maximum loaded, 44,800 lb.

Dimensions: Rotor diameter (each), 60 ft. 0 in.; fuselage length, 51 ft. 0 in.; overall height, 18 ft. 6½ in.

Notes: First flown on October 14, 1967, the CH-47C supplants in production the CH-47B from which it differs solely in the model of the T55 turboshaft installed, the earlier variant of the Chinook having 2,850 s.h.p. T55-L-7C engines. The more powerful engines result in a 25% increase in payload capability and enable the CH-47C to transport loads weighing up to 23,400 lb. The U.S. Army took delivery of the first CH-47C in March 1968, and by the end of 1968 more than 500 Chinooks had been delivered, the first having entered service in 1963. An armed version of the earlier CH-47A has been tested in Vietnam.

BOEING-VERTOL CH-46D SEA KNIGHT

Country of Origin: U.S.A.
Type: Medium Transport and Assault Helicopter.
Power Plants: Two General Electric T58-GE-10 turbo-shafts each rated at 1,400 s.h.p.
Performance: Maximum speed (at 20,800 lb.), 166 m.p.h. at sea level; long range cruising speed (at 23,000 lb.), 153 m.p.h.; tactical radius, 115 mls.; maximum inclined climb rate (at 20,800 lb.), 1,900 ft./min.; hovering ceiling (at 20,800 lb. out of ground effect), 5,600 ft.
Weights: Empty, 13,067 lb.; max. loaded, 23,000 lb.
Dimensions: Rotor diameter (each), 51 ft. 0 in.; fuselage length, 44 ft. 10 in.; overall height, 16 ft. 11½ in.
Notes: The CH-46D and UH-46D are respectively U.S. Marine Corps logistic support and assault, and U.S. Navy medium utility and transport helicopters, these differing from the earlier CH-46A and UH-46A in having uprated turboshafts, cambered rotor blades with formation tip lights, provision for armour and armament. The CH-46D may accommodate up to 25 troops or 15 casualty litters and two medical attendants. More than 475 CH/UH-46s have been delivered, and licence manufacture of the basic Model 107 is undertaken in Japan (illustrated).

262

BÖLKOW BÖ 105

Country of Origin: Federal Germany.
Type: Light Utility Helicopter.
Power Plants: Two MAN Turbo-6022-701-A3 turbo-shafts each rated at 375 s.h.p.
Performance: (Estimated) Maximum speed, 155 m.p.h.; maximum cruising speed, 143 m.p.h.; maximum inclined climb rate 2,060 ft./min.; hovering ceiling (in ground effect), 15,090 ft.; (out of ground effect), 11,480 ft.; service ceiling, 18,700 ft.; normal range, 440 mls., (with auxiliary fuel), 858 mls. at 6,600 ft.
Weights: Empty, 2,360 lb.; loaded, 4,410 lb.
Dimensions: Rotor diameter, 32 ft. 2 in.; fuselage length, 28 ft. 0½ in.; overall height, 9 ft. 9⅜ in.
Notes: The first prototype of the Bö 105 powered by a pair of Allison 250-C18 turboshafts and equipped with a Westland Scout articulated blade rotor system was destroyed as a result of resonance during ground trials. The similarly-powered second prototype flew on February 16, 1967, and differed in having the Bölkow rigid rotor system with lightweight glass-fibre-reinforced plastic blades. The third prototype, flown December 20, 1967, is described above; two pre-production examples will fly during 1969, and production deliveries (by SIAT) will begin 1970.

ENSTROM F-28A

Country of Origin: U.S.A.
Type: Three-seat Light Utility Helicopter.
Power Plant: One Lycoming HIO-360-C1B four-cylinder horizontally-opposed engine rated at 205 h.p.
Performance: Maximum speed, 100 m.p.h.; Maximum cruising speed, 98 m.p.h.; maximum inclined climb rate, 1,025 ft./min.; hovering ceiling (in ground effect), 4,900 ft., (out of ground effect), 2,400 ft.; maximum range, 235 mls.
Weights: Empty, 1,430 lb.; maximum loaded, 2,150 lb.
Dimensions: Rotor diameter, 32 ft. 0 in.; fuselage length, 28 ft. 1 in.; overall height, 9 ft. 1 in.
Notes: Production successor to the F-28, the F-28A was introduced late in 1967; deliveries commencing during the summer of 1968. Further development of the basic design of which production is planned for the second half of 1969 is the T-28A which is to be powered by a 220 s.h.p. Garrett–AiResearch TSE36-1 turboshaft. Flight testing of an F-28 helicopter with a TSE36-1 turboshaft was initiated mid-1968, and production of the T-28A is expected to attain 15 per month by 1970. The first of two F-28 production prototypes flew on May 27, 1962, and production rate of the F-28A helicopter during 1968 averaged one machine per month.

FAIRCHILD HILLER FH 1100

Country of Origin: U.S.A.
Type: Four-seat Utility Helicopter.
Power Plant: One Allison 250-C18 turboshaft rated at 275 s.h.p.
Performance: Maximum speed, 127 m.p.h. at sea level; maximum cruising speed, 127 m.p.h. at 5,000 ft.; maximum inclined climb rate (at 2,530 lb.), 1,690 ft./min.; hovering ceiling (in ground effect), 15,950 ft., (out of ground effect), 11,100 ft.; service ceiling, 16,400 ft.; maximum range, 410 mls.
Weights: Empty, 1,395 lb.; max. loaded, 2,750 lb.
Dimensions: Rotor diameter, 35 ft. 5 in.; fuselage length, 29 ft. 9½ in.; overall height, 9 ft. 4¾ in.
Notes: The FH 1100 is a commercial derivative of the OH-5A which was the runner-up in the U.S. Army's first LOH (Light Observation Helicopter) contest, and the first production model was rolled out in April 1966. A somewhat more sophisticated helicopter than the Hughes winning entry in the initial LOH contest, the FH 1100 has hydraulically-boosted cyclic and collective pitch controls, and has been test flown in level flight at 160 m.p.h., although for maximum turbine efficiency cruise and red-lined speeds are identical at 127 m.p.h. Basically a four-seater, the FH 1100 is also available in five-seater form.

HUGHES MODEL 500 (OH-6A) CAYUSE

Country of Origin: U.S.A.
Type: Four-seat Light Observation and Utility Helicopter.
Power Plant: One Allison T63-A-5A turboshaft rated at 252 s.h.p.
Performance: Maximum speed (at 2,400 lb.), 143 m.p.h. at sea level; economical cruising speed, 134 m.p.h.; maximum inclined climb rate, 1,560 ft./min.; hovering ceiling (out of ground effect), 7,600 ft.; service ceiling, 15,550 ft.; range, 413 mls.
Weights: Empty, 1,156 lb.; normal loaded, 2,400 lb.; maximum overload, 2,700 lb.
Dimensions: Rotor diameter, 26 ft. 3 in.; fuselage length, 23 ft. 0 in.; overall height, 8 ft. 8½ in.
Notes: The Model 500 was, in its military form (to which the above specification applies), pronounced winner of the U.S. Army's first LOH (Light Observation Helicopter) contest in 1965, and deliveries commenced in September 1966, total orders for 1,415 having been placed by the beginning of 1969. Licence manufacture of the OH-6A is being undertaken in Japan, after delivery of 17 helicopters to Kawasaki by the parent company late 1968. The commercial Model 500 is basically a five-seater.
266

KAMAN UH-2C SEASPRITE

Country of Origin: U.S.A.

Type: Rescue and Utility Helicopter.

Power Plants: Two General Electric T58-GE-8B turboshafts each rated at 1,250 s.h.p. but flat-rated to provide a maximum allowable total of 1,685 s.h.p.

Performance: Maximum speed, 158 m.p.h. at sea level; normal cruising speed, 150 m.p.h.; maximum inclined climb rate, 1,920 ft./min.; hovering ceiling (in ground effect), 18,400 ft., (out of ground effect), 16,050 ft.; normal range, 425 mls.

Weights: Empty, 7,350 lb.; normal loaded, 9,951 lb.; maximum overload, 11,000 lb.

Dimensions: Rotor diameter, 44 ft. 0 in.; fuselage length, 37 ft. 9½ in.; overall height, 15 ft. 5 in.

Notes: The UH-2C is a twin-engined conversion of the single-engined UH-2A and -2B, 88 of the former and 96 of the latter having been built, and some 130 of these being scheduled for conversion, deliveries to the U.S. Navy of the converted helicopter having begun in May 1967. The UH-2C has a flight crew of two and can accommodate a maximum of 11 passengers, and 12 of the UH-2C conversions are being completed as gunships, with a chin-mounted 7·62-mm. rotary machine gun, and two similar weapons mounted in waist positions, plus additional fuel tank protection.

267

KAMOV KA-25K (HORMONE)

Country of Origin: U.S.S.R.
Type: General-purpose and Utility Helicopter.
Power Plants: Two Glushenkov turboshafts each rated at 900 e.h.p.
Performance: Maximum speed, 137 m.p.h.; normal cruising speed, 121 m.p.h.; normal range (with 12 passengers), 248 mls.; range with auxiliary fuel, 404 mls.; range with 4,410-lb. slung load, 31 mls.
Weights: Normal loaded, 15,653 lb.; maximum loaded, 16,094 lb.
Dimensions: Rotor diameter (each), 51 ft. 7½ in.; fuselage length, 32 ft. 3 in.; overall height, 17 ft. 7⅓ in.
Notes: A multi-purpose helicopter evolved from the Ka-20 anti-submarine warfare helicopter, the Ka-25K was under test in prototype form in 1967. Capable of accommodating up to 12 passengers or a maximum freight load of 4,410 lb., the latter being slung beneath the fuselage, the Ka-25K featured an hydraulic winch, the winch operator being accommodated in an aft-facing glazed gondola beneath the fuselage nose. The turboshaft engines are mounted side-by-side above the cabin. An assault transport version is employed by the Soviet Navy aboard the helicopter carriers *Moskva* and *Leningradskii.*

KAMOV KA-26 (HOODLUM)

Country of Origin: U.S.S.R.
Type: Light Utility Helicopter.
Power Plants: Two Vedeneev M-14V-26 air-cooled radial engines each rated at 325 h.p.
Performance: Maximum speed, 106 m.p.h.; cruising speed, 84 m.p.h.; economic cruising speed, 62 m.p.h.; hovering ceiling at 6,614 lb. (in ground effect), 4,068 ft., (out of ground effect), 2,625 ft.; service ceiling, 9,843 ft.; range (with seven passengers), 250 mls. at 1,640 ft., with auxiliary tanks, 746 mls.
Weights: Operational empty, 4,300 lb.; loaded, 6,614 lb., (agricultural version), 6,966 lb.
Dimensions: Rotor diameter (each), 42 ft. 8 in.; fuselage length, 25 ft. 5½ in.; overall height, 13 ft. 3 in.
Notes: The Ka-26, which appeared in 1965, is a multipurpose helicopter which features a removable cabin for six passengers, two casualty stretchers, two sitting casualties and a medical attendant, or freight. The passenger cabin may be replaced by an open platform for bulky cargo loads, and an agricultural version can carry 1,984 lb. of dry chemicals or a tank for an equivalent quantity of liquid chemical. The plastic and fibreglass rotor blades are interchangeable. Production deliveries began in 1966.

269

LOCKHEED AH-56A CHEYENNE

Country of Origin: U.S.A.

Type: Two-seat Attack and Escort Helicopter.

Power Plant: One General Electric T64-GE-16 turbo-shaft rated at 3,435 s.h.p.

Performance: (Estimated) Maximum speed, 253 m.p.h. at sea level; cruising speed, 242 m.p.h. at 5,000 ft., 236 m.p.h. at 10,000 ft.; maximum inclined climb rate, 3,420 ft./min.; hovering ceiling (out of ground effect), 10,600 ft.; service ceiling, 26,000 ft.; maximum range 875 mls.; ferry range, 2,890 mls. at 194 m.p.h.

Weights: Empty, 11,718 lb.; design loaded, 16,995 lb.; VTOL overload, 22,000 lb.; ferry overload (STOL), 28,000 lb.

Dimensions: Rotor diameter, 50 ft. 4¾ in.; wing span, 26 ft. 7¼ in.; wing area, 260 sq. ft.; fuselage length, 54 ft. 8 in.; overall height, 13 ft. 7¼ in.

Armament: One 7·62-mm. Minigun or 40-mm. grenade launcher in nose turret, and additional weapons on six 2,000-lb. capacity external pylons.

Notes: The Cheyenne was flown for the first time on September 21, 1967, and all 10 prototypes were completed by mid-1968. U.S. Army evaluation commencing early in 1969. Between 500 and 1,000 AH-56As are to be acquired by the U.S. Army, an initial order for 375 having been placed early in 1968.

MIL MI-2 (HOPLITE)

Country of Origin: U.S.S.R. (Licence-built in Poland).
Type: Light Utility Helicopter.
Power Plants: Two Izotov GTD-350 turboshafts each rated at 400 s.h.p.
Performance: Maximum speed, 137 m.p.h.; economical cruising speed, 112 m.p.h.; hovering ceiling (out of ground effect), 4,760 ft.; service ceiling, 13,120 ft.; range (with 1,984-lb. payload), 68 mls., (with auxiliary fuel), 444 mls.
Weight: Maximum loaded, 7,715 lb.
Dimensions: Rotor diameter, 47 ft. 6¾ in.; fuselage length, 39 ft. 2 in.; overall height, 12 ft. 3½ in.
Notes: The Mi-2, is currently in large-scale production under licence in Poland by WSK Swidnik where it is being produced in four versions; a seven-passenger model, an agricultural model fitted with two external containers for a maximum of 1,984 lb. of dry chemicals, a freighter version with a 264-lb. capacity winch and the ability to carry 1,543 lb. internally or 1,764 lb. externally, and an ambulance with accommodation for four stretchers and one attendant. Initially flown in 1963, the Mi-2 has established two F.A.I.-recognised speed records for helicopters in its class, the latest, established on June 20, 1965, being 167·2 m.p.h.

MIL MI-6 (HOOK)

Country of Origin: U.S.S.R.

Type: Heavy Transport Helicopter.

Power Plants: Two Soloviev D-25V turboshafts each rated at 5,500 s.h.p.

Performance: Maximum speed, 186 m.p.h.; normal cruising speed, 155 m.p.h.; range (with 13,228-lb. payload), 394 mls., (with 17,637-lb. payload), 385 mls., (with 26,455-lb. payload), 124 mls.; maximum range, 652 mls.; service ceiling, 14,764 ft.

Weights: Empty, 59,525 lb.; normal loaded, 89,287 lb.; maximum loaded, 93,696 lb.

Dimensions: Rotor diameter, 114 ft. 10 in.; fuselage length, 122 ft. 6 in.; overall height, 40 ft. 6 in.

Notes: First flown in 1957 and manufactured in some numbers since 1959, the Mi-6 is currently the world's largest helicopter, and is in service in both civil and military forms, the latter having been delivered to the U.A.R., North Vietnam, and Indonesia. The civil version can accommodate 65 passengers, and as an ambulance 41 casualty stretchers may be carried. The military version can accommodate 70 fully-equipped paratroops. Auxiliary wings are fitted to off-load the main rotor in cruising flight, but these may be removed when the Mi-6 is operated as a flying crane or as a water-bomber for fire-fighting.

272

MIL MI-8 (HIP)

Country of Origin: U.S.S.R.

Type: Commercial Transport Helicopter.

Power Plants: Two Izotov TB-2-117 turboshafts each rated at 1,500 s.h.p.

Performance: Maximum speed, 155 m.p.h.; maximum cruising speed, 143 m.p.h.; normal cruising speed, 125 m.p.h.; range (with 6,614-lb. payload), 248 mls., (with 8,818-lb. payload), 62 mls.; maximum range, 280 mls., (with auxiliary fuel), 435 mls.; service ceiling (at 24,251 lb.), 13,120 ft.

Weights: Empty, 15,800 lb.; normal loaded, 24,251 lb.; maximum loaded, 26,455 lb.

Dimensions: Rotor diameter, 56 ft. 5 in.; fuselage length, 49 ft. 2½ in.; overall height, 14 ft. 9 in.

Notes: Evolved from the piston-engined Mi-4 but retaining few interchangeable components in its definitive production form, the Mi-8 is being manufactured in two versions, one accommodating up to 28 passengers and the other being intended for the freight transportation role with a maximum cargo load of 8,818 lb. Either passenger or freight version may be converted for the ambulance role with 12 casualty stretchers and one medical attendant. A controllable winch and underside cargo hook for lifting slung loads up to 5,500 lb. may be fitted.

MIL MI-10K (HARKE)

Country of Origin: U.S.S.R.

Type: Heavy Crane-type Helicopter.

Power Plants: Two Soloviev D25V turboshafts each rated at 5,500 s.h.p.

Performance: (Specification is applicable to standard Mi-10 but, apart from range, is also generally applicable to the Mi-10K) Maximum speed (with empty cargo platform), 124 m.p.h., (with high-density platform load weighing 26,455 lb.), 112 m.p.h.; range (with 26,455-lb. load), 155 mls.; maximum range (with auxiliary fuel), 391 mls.; service ceiling, 9,842 ft.

Weights: (Mi-10) Empty, 59,525 lb.; maximum loaded 95,790 lb.

Dimensions: Rotor diameter, 82 ft. 0 in.; overall length 137 ft. 5 in.; overall height (Mi-10), 32 ft. 6 in.

Notes: The Mi-10K, which was still undergoing development in 1966, is a derivative of the production Mi-10 (see 1966 edition) in which a supplementary cockpit with full controls is provided beneath the front fuselage, the height of the undercarriage has been reduced, and a maximum slung load is increased to 24,250 lb.; this being scheduled to be raised to 30,864 lb. with an increase in rated power of the D25V turboshafts to 6,500 s.h.p.

SIAI-MARCHETTI SH-4

Country of Origin: Italy.

Type: Three-seat Light Utility Helicopter.

Power Plant: One Franklin 6A-350-D or -D1 six-cylinder horizontally-opposed engine derated to 160 h.p.

Performance: Maximum speed, 100 m.p.h. at sea level; maximum cruising speed, 87 m.p.h.; economic cruising speed, 80 m.p.h.; maximum inclined climb rate, 1,140 ft./min.; hovering ceiling (in ground effect), 12,300 ft., (out of ground effect), 6,730 ft.; service ceiling, 13,155 ft.; maximum range, 186 mls.

Weights: Empty, 1,120 lb.; maximum loaded, 1,900 lb.

Dimensions: Rotor diameter, 29 ft. 7½ in.; fuselage length, 25 ft. 1¼ in.; overall height, 9 ft. 9¼ in.

Notes: The first prototype SH-4 helicopter was flown in March 1965, this being followed by five production examples completed in 1967–68, but future production plans were uncertain at the time of closing for press. Design emphasis has been placed on simplicity of operation, ease of maintenance and low initial cost. The standard tubular-steel skid undercarriage may be replaced by multi-cell floats, agricultural spraying equipment may be fitted, and an external stretcher pod may be attached to the port side of the fuselage. An external sling can support loads up to 440 lb.

SIKORSKY HH-3E

Country of Origin: U.S.A.

Type: Medium Rescue Helicopter.

Power Plants: Two General Electric T58-GE-5 turbo-shafts each rated at 1,500 s.h.p.

Performance: Maximum speed, 165 m.p.h.; maximum cruising speed, 154 m.p.h.; maximum inclined climb rate, 1,520 ft./min.; service ceiling, 11,700 ft.; range (with external jettisonable fuel tanks), 748 mls.

Weights: Empty, 14,426 lb.; normal loaded, 19,500 lb.; maximum, 22,050 lb.

Dimensions: Rotor diameter, 62 ft. 0 in.; fuselage length, 56 ft. 7 in.; overall height, 18 ft. 1 in.

Notes: The HH-3E is an armoured rescue variant of the S-61R, and differs from the U.S.A.F.'s CH-3E support transport helicopter in having self-sealing fuel tanks, a retractable flight refuelling probe, defensive armament and a rescue hoist. The HH-3F of the U.S. Coast Guard is similar but does not have armour, armament or self-sealing tanks. It features sophisticated electronic gear for automatic navigation, communications, and search and weather radar. The HH-3F can carry 20 passengers or nine casualty stretchers, and the CH-3E can accommodate up to 30 troops or 5,000 lb. of cargo.

SIKORSKY HH-53B

Country of Origin: U.S.A.

Type: Combat Aircrew Rescue Helicopter.

Power Plants: Two General Electric T64-GE-3 turbo-shafts each rated at 3,080 s.h.p.

Performance: Maximum speed, 195 m.p.h.; cruising speed, 172 m.p.h.; maximum inclined climb rate, 1,625 ft./min.; service ceiling, 18,550 ft.; maximum range, 806 mls.

Weights: Empty, 23,125 lb.; normal loaded, 35,000 lb.; maximum overload, 42,000 lb.

Dimensions: Rotor diameter, 72 ft. 2¾ in.; fuselage length, 67 ft. 2¼ in.; overall height, 24 ft. 10½ in.

Notes: Flown for the first time on March 15, 1967, the HH-53B is the U.S.A.F. combat aircrew rescue version of the S-65, and features a retractable flight refuelling probe, jettisonable auxiliary fuel tanks, rescue hoist and defensive armament. Armament comprises three 7·62-mm. Miniguns firing from a port forward window, a starboard door and the tail hatch. The CH-53A Sea Stallion is a U.S. Marine Corps heavy assault helicopter which can accommodate up to 37 combat-equipped troops, 24 casualty stretchers, or such loads as two Hawk missiles or a 105-mm. howitzer and carriage. The current production model, the HH-53C, has 3,435 s.h.p. T64-GE-7 turboshafts.

277

SUD-AVIATION SA-321 SUPER FRELON

Country of Origin: France.

Type: Medium Transport and (SA-321G) Anti-submarine Warfare Helicopter.

Power Plants: Three Turboméca Turmo IIIC.3 turboshafts each rated at 1,500 s.h.p.

Performance: Maximum speed (at 24,250 lb.), 158 m.p.h. at sea level; maximum cruising speed, 149 m.p.h.; maximum inclined climb rate, 1,475 ft./min.; service ceiling, 10,800 ft.; range (with 5,925-lb. payload), 234 mls.; ferry range, 733 mls.

Weights: Empty, 14,640 lb.; normal loaded, 24,250 lb.; maximum loaded, 26,455 lb.

Dimensions: Rotor diameter, 62 ft. 0 in.; fuselage length, 62 ft. 3 in.; overall height, 16 ft. 2½ in.

Notes: Two prototypes and four pre-production examples of the SA-321 Super Frelon (Super Hornet) are currently being followed by 38 production examples, including 12 of the non-amphibious SA-321K transport version (illustrated) for the Israeli Defence Force. The amphibious ASW version, the SA-321G, is being manufactured for France's Aéronavale (12) and for the South African Air Force (16) as the SA-321L, this having Sylph radars in the outrigger floats, dunking sonar, and up to four homing torpedoes and other ASW stores.

278

SUD-AVIATION SA-330 PUMA

Country of Origin: France.

Type: Tactical Assault and Transport Helicopter.

Power Plants: Two Turboméca Turmo IIIC.4 turbo-shafts each rated at 1,300 s.h.p.

Performance: Maximum speed, 174 m.p.h. at sea level; normal cruising speed, 157 m.p.h.; maximum inclined climb rate, 1,635 ft./min.; hovering ceiling (out of ground effect), 12,800 ft.; service ceiling, 18,300 ft.; range (with 3,858-lb. payload), 230 mls.; ferry range, 870 mls. at 4,900 ft.

Weights: Empty, 7,187 lb.; normal loaded, 13,220 lb.; maximum loaded, 14,110 lb.

Dimensions: Rotor diameter, 49 ft. 2½ in.; fuselage length, 45 ft. 6 in.; overall height, 17 ft. 0 in.

Notes: The SA-330 has been developed specifically to a French Army requirement, and quantity production was initiated in 1967. The SA-330 has a crew of two and accommodates a maximum of 12 fully-equipped troops, and eight test and evaluation examples were built for the flight development programme, the first having flown on April 15, 1965. The first production SA-330 flew in September 1968, and plans currently call for the manufacture of 130 SA-330s for the French Army in collaboration with Westland, the British company assembling 48 for the R.A.F.

SUD-AVIATION SA-341

Country of Origin: France.

Type: Light Observation Helicopter.

Power Plant: One Turboméca Astazou IIN.2 turbo-shaft rated at 600 s.h.p.

Performance: (At 3,530 lb.) Maximum speed, 169 m.p.h. at sea level; economical cruising speed, 137 m.p.h.; maximum inclined climb rate, 1,650 ft./min.; hovering ceiling (in ground effect), 12,465 ft., (out of ground effect), 10,500 ft.; range, 426 mls.

Weights: Empty, 1,765 lb.; loaded, 3,530 lb.; maximum overload, 3,750 lb.

Dimensions: Rotor diameter, 34 ft. 5½ in.; fuselage length, 30 ft. 10½ in.; overall height, 9 ft. 8½ in.

Notes: The SA-341 is being manufactured under a joint Anglo-French programme as the standard light observation helicopter for both the British and French armed forces, the former having a requirement for some 600 and the latter approximately 100. The SA-341 is the production derivative of the SA-340, two prototypes of which have been tested, the first having flown on April 7, 1967, and the second (illustrated), featuring the 13-blade shrouded anti-torque rotor to be utilised by the SA-341, flying on August 2, 1968. Four pre-production SA-341s are being built, and the first production helicopter is to fly mid-1970.

VFW H3

Country of Origin: Federal Germany.
Type: Three-seat Compound Helicopter.
Power Plants: Two Budworth Puffin turbo-compressors each rated at 200 h.p.
Performance: (Estimated) Maximum speed, 155 m.p.h.; cruising speed, 149 m.p.h.; maximum inclined climb rate, 2,940 ft./min.; service ceiling, 13,250 ft.; maximum range, 310 mls.
Weights: Empty, 1,069 lb.; loaded, 2,127 lb.
Dimensions: Rotor diameter, 28 ft. $6\frac{1}{2}$ in.; fuselage length, 23 ft. $1\frac{1}{2}$ in.; overall height 8 ft. 2 in.
Notes: The VFW H3, the prototype of which was completed on October 6, 1968, and was scheduled to commence its flight test programme before the end of the year, is intended to combine the advantages of the gyroplane with those of the helicopter, the turbo-compressors driving the rotor for vertical take-off, hovering and landing, compressed air being ejected from blade-tip nozzles, or driving two shrouded fans via a pneumatic transmission, the intention being to attach these fans to the fuselage sides immediately aft of the cabin. The H3 will be able to perform jump-start take-offs with free-wheeling rotor, using a pre-take-off rotor spin-up technique, or will take-off vertically with all power being fed to the rotor tips.

281

WESTLAND SCOUT A.H. MK. 1

Country of Origin: United Kingdom.
Type: Light Utility Helicopter.
Power Plant: One Rolls-Royce Bristol Nimbus 102 turboshaft rated at 685 s.h.p.
Performance: Maximum speed, 132 m.p.h.; maximum cruising speed, 122 m.p.h.; maximum inclined climb rate, 1,670 ft./min.; hovering ceiling (in ground effect), 15,400 ft., (out of ground effect), 10,000 ft.; maximum range (with standard fuel), 322 mls.
Weights: Empty, 3,184 lb.; maximum loaded, 5,300 lb.
Dimensions: Rotor diameter, 32 ft. 3 in.; fuselage length, 30 ft. 7½ in.; overall height, 8 ft. 11 in.
Notes: Derived from the same basic design as the Wasp A.S. Mk. 1, the Scout is currently in production for and in service with the British Army, two have been supplied to the Royal Australian Navy, one to the Bahrein State Police, two to the Uganda Police Air Wing, and three to the Royal Jordanian Arab Army. For the ambulance role two casualty stretchers may be accommodated, and a sling for external freight and a power-operated rescue hoist may be fitted. The Scout may also carry wire-guided missiles such as the Nord SS.11, and up to five passengers may be carried. A number of components are similar to those of Wasp.

WESTLAND SEA KING H.A.S. Mk. 1

Country of Origin: United Kingdom (U.S. licence).
Type: Amphibious Anti-submarine Warfare Helicopter.
Power Plants: Two Rolls-Royce Gnome H.1400 turboshafts each rated at 1,500 s.h.p.
Performance: (At 20,500 lb.) Maximum speed, 161 m.p.h.; maximum cruising speed, 158 m.p.h.; maximum inclined climb rate, 3,000 ft./min.; tactical radius with 7,000-lb. payload, 57 mls.; maximum range, 690 mls.; typical ensurance (A.S.W. mission), 2·5 hr. on station at 115-mile radius.
Weights: Basic, 12,170 lb.; maximum, 20,500 lb.
Dimensions: Rotor diameter, 62 ft. 0 in.; fuselage length, 54 ft. 9 in.; overall height, 16 ft. 10 in.
Notes: Westland is manufacturing an anglicised version of the Sikorsky SH-3D Sea King (see 1968 edition) for the Royal Navy, some 60 helicopters of this type having been ordered for 1969-70 delivery, the first having been scheduled to commence its flight test programme mid-December 1968. Four Sikorsky-built SH-3D helicopters have been utilised to test the all-British systems and components (sonar, doppler, radar, radio altimeter, flight control and compass systems). The first SH-3D re-engined with Gnome turboshafts flew on September 8, 1967.

WESTLAND WASP A.S. MK. 1

Country of Origin: United Kingdom.
Type: Anti-submarine Warfare Helicopter.
Power Plant: One Rolls-Royce Bristol Nimbus 503 turboshaft rated at 710 s.h.p.
Performance: Maximum speed, 121 m.p.h.; cruising speed, 110 m.p.h.; maximum inclined climb rate, 1,440 ft./min.; hovering ceiling (in ground effect), 12,500 ft., (out of ground effect), 8,800 ft.; maximum range, 303 mls.
Weights: Empty, 3,452 lb.; maximum loaded, 5,500 lb.
Dimensions: Rotor diameter, 32 ft. 3 in., fuselage length, 30 ft. 5¾ in., overall height, 9 ft. 9 in.
Notes: The Wasp A.S. Mk. 1 currently serves with the Royal Navy in the anti-submarine weapon-carrying role, operating from platforms aboard frigates equipped with long-range asdic. In this role the Wasp is normally crewed by a single pilot and carries two 270-lb. torpedoes. Dual controls may be fitted for the training role, and four passengers may be carried. The Wasp has been supplied to the Brazilian, Netherlands, New Zealand and South African navies. A specially designed undercarriage incorporating fully castoring, lockable wheels permits normal operation aboard ship in heavy seas, and a power hoist, operated by the pilot or a crewman, is installed for rescue missions.

284

INDEX OF AIRCRAFT TYPES

285